T0318917

Cambridge Elements ≡

Elements of Paleontology
edited by
Colin D. Sumrall
University of Tennessee

THE ECOLOGY OF BIOTIC INTERACTIONS IN ECHINOIDS

Modern Insights into Ancient Interactions

Elizabeth Petsios
Baylor University

Lyndsey Farrar
*Florida Museum of Natural History,
University of Florida*

Shamindri Tennakoon
Hendrix College

Fatemah Jamal
Kuwait University

Roger W. Portell
*Florida Museum of Natural History,
University of Florida*

Michał Kowalewski
*Florida Museum of Natural History,
University of Florida*

Carrie L. Tyler
University of Nevada

Paleontological
S O C I E T Y

CAMBRIDGE
UNIVERSITY PRESS

CAMBRIDGE
UNIVERSITY PRESS

Shaftesbury Road, Cambridge CB2 8EA, United Kingdom

One Liberty Plaza, 20th Floor, New York, NY 10006, USA

477 Williamstown Road, Port Melbourne, VIC 3207, Australia

314–321, 3rd Floor, Plot 3, Splendor Forum, Jasola District Centre,
New Delhi – 110025, India

103 Penang Road, #05–06/07, Visioncrest Commercial, Singapore 238467

Cambridge University Press is part of Cambridge University Press & Assessment,
a department of the University of Cambridge.

We share the University's mission to contribute to society through the pursuit of
education, learning and research at the highest international levels of excellence.

www.cambridge.org
Information on this title: www.cambridge.org/9781108810067

DOI: 10.1017/9781108893510

First published 2023

A catalogue record for this publication is available from the British Library

ISBN 978-1-108-81006-7 Paperback
ISSN 2517-780X (online)
ISSN 2517-7796 (print)

The Ecology of Biotic Interactions in Echinoids

Modern Insights into Ancient Interactions

Elements of Paleontology

DOI: 10.1017/9781108893510
First published online: November 2023

Elizabeth Petsios
Baylor University

Lyndsey Farrar
Florida Museum of Natural History, University of Florida

Shamindri Tennakoon
Hendrix College

Fatemah Jamal
Kuwait University

Roger W. Portell
Florida Museum of Natural History, University of Florida

Michał Kowalewski
Florida Museum of Natural History, University of Florida

Carrie L. Tyler
University of Nevada

Author for correspondence: Elizabeth Petsios, Elizabeth_Petsios@Baylor.edu

Abstract: Organisms interacting with echinoids are common and produce diverse traces that are often distinctive and can be preserved in the fossil record. Thus, echinoids provide a wealth of information regarding the role of biotic interactions as drivers of ecological and morphological adaptations over macroevolutionary timescales. Studies documenting interactions with echinoids and the resulting traces have become more numerous. This Element reviews the ecologies of skeletal trace-producing interactions on echinoids in modern ecosystems and the recognition of those biogenic traces in the fossil record. The authors explore diversification and morphological trends in Meso-Cenozoic echinoid clades and associated predator and parasite groups in the context of selective pressures brought about by the evolution of these biotic interactions. Their intent is that this review promotes additional studies documenting the intensity of biotic interactions with echinoids in both Recent and fossil assemblages and highlights their potential to advance our understanding of ecosystem functioning and evolution. This title is also available as Open Access on Cambridge Core.

Keywords: biotic interactions, echinoids, paleoecology, trace fossils, predator–prey interactions

ISBNs: 9781108810067 (PB), 9781108893510 (OC)
ISSNs: 2517-780X (online), 2517-7796 (print)

Contents

1 Introduction

Several macroevolutionary hypotheses, including van Valen's (1973) Red Queen and Vermeij's (1977, 1987) Escalation, posit that ecological interactions are an important evolutionary force. However, our current understanding of the effects of biotic interactions on evolution relies predominantly on a single taxonomic group, mollusks, and their predators. Drill hole frequencies on mollusk prey have classically been used as a proxy for predation intensity experienced by ancient species and communities (e.g., Vermeij, 1983; Kowalewski et al., 1998; Kelley and Hansen, 2003; Klompmaker et al., 2019), as they are readily identifiable and quantifiable. Several ecological and morphological trends in marine invertebrate groups have been interpreted as adaptations in response to the selective pressures of biotic interactions, most commonly trends observed during the Mesozoic Marine Revolution. These include but are not limited to increasing shell ribosity and spinosity (Signor and Brett, 1984; Harper and Skelton, 1993), increased prevalence of encrusting and cementing prey (Hautmann, 2004; Tackett, 2016), increased mobility (Aberhan et al., 2006), and increased frequency and depth of infaunalization (Buatois et al., 2022). If biotic interactions are an important cause of evolutionary change, we should also be able to identify patterns in interaction intensity and diversity in other groups, such as echinoids. Echinoids are important prey for several predatory groups in Recent marine ecosystems, including crabs, birds, fish, gastropods, and other echinoderms (see Kowalewski and Nebelsick, 2003; Farrar et al., 2020 and references therein); however, evolutionary trends in response to predation have received relatively little attention (but see Kier 1974, 1982; Petsios et al., 2021).

Predators and parasites of echinoids include gastropods (Moore 1956; Chesher, 1969; Hughes and Hughes, 1971; Hendler, 1977; Gladfelter 1978; Serafy, 1979; Warén, 1980a; Warén, 1980b; Hughes, 1981; Kier, 1981; Warén et al. 1983; Fujioka, 1985; Alekseev and Endelman, 1989; Levitan and Genovese, 1989; Warén and Moolenbeek, 1989; Warén and Mifsud, 1990; Warén and Crossland, 1991; Crossland et al., 1991, 1993; McClintock and Marion, 1993; Oliverio et al., 1994; Rinaldi and Malacologico, 1994; Warén et al., 1994; McClanahan, 1999; Nebelsick and Kowalewski, 1999; Ceranka and Złotnik, 2003; Vaïtilingon et al., 2004; Złotnik and Ceranka, 2005a, b; Neumann and Wisshak 2009; Meadows et al., 2015), polychaetes (Wisshak and Neumann, 2006), crustaceans (Tegner and Levin, 1983; Smith, 1984; Wirtz et al., 2009) including barnacles (Madsen and Wolff, 1965; Cross and Rose, 1994; Donovan et al., 2016) and copepods (Margara, 1946; Roman, 1954), echinoderms (Merril and Hobson, 1970; Serafy, 1979), fish (Borszcz and Zatoń, 2013; Wilson et al., 2014) and other vertebrates, such as turtles, birds, and sea otters (see references in Smith, 1984; Hendler et al., 1995; and Nebelsick et al., 1998) (Table 1). Herein, we review biogenic skeletal traces found in both fossil and Recent echinoids, and the ecological interactions that are known or are interpreted to have caused them. We focus on interactions in Recent ecosystems that produce traces that are likely to be recognized in the fossil record, namely traces left on parts of the echinoid that are more likely to enter the fossil record (such as the test and spines) and that are readily diagnostic as having been produced by specific types of ecological interactions. We briefly explore important symbiotic interactions on Recent echinoid populations that are unlikely to be preserved in the fossil record, so-called invisible interactions. Finally, we review taxonomic diversification trends across the Meso-Cenozoic in regular and "irregular" echinoids, along with some of their common predators and parasites.

2 Predators

Multiple vertebrate and invertebrate groups prey on both infaunal and epifaunal echinoids. Given their vastly different life habits, regular, and irregular echinoids employ different antipredatory strategies, and yet several predator groups prey on both regular and irregular echinoids alike (Nebelsick et al., 1998). Skeletal damage caused by these predators has varying degrees of likelihood of preservation and identification in the fossil record, dependent upon the extent of the damage, the lethality of it, and the setting in which the attack takes place (Tyler et al., 2018).

2.1 Whole-Test Crushing Predation

Crushing predation is differentiated herein from margin damage predation (see Section 2.2) in that crushing predation causes damage to all or most of the test, such that survival and recovery of the prey is not possible. Fish are a major group of predators of echinoids (Kowalewski and Nebelsick, 2003; Nebelsick and Mancosu, 2022). Many groups of teleost fish prey on regular and irregular echinoids and utilize varying strategies leaving behind different traces of test damage. In Recent ecosystems, for example, the Mediterranean urchin *Sphaerechinus granularis* is preyed on by sparid fish resulting in large, gaping wounds from these lethal attacks. Scratch marks, spine damage, and semicircular indentations are visible at the edges of the wounds (Sievers and Nebelsick, 2018). Stingrays have been observed preying on the large spatangoid echinoid *Meoma ventricosa* in San Salvador, Bahamas, resulting in test damage and substantial plate loss on the oral side with no observed spine damage (Grun, 2016). Other vertebrates, such as turtles, seabirds, and marine mammals also

Table 1 List of echinoid associates, ecology of interaction, and known traces

Predator/Symbiont	Interaction type	Trace producing	Fossil examples	Source
Vertebrates				
Fish	Predation	Crushing	Yes	Neumann and Hampe, 2018; Borszcz and Zatón, 2013; Wilson et al., 2014; Nebelsick and Mancosu, 2022
		Margin Damage	Yes	Frazer et al., 1991; Kowalewski and Nebelsick, 2003; Kurz, 1995; Nebelsick, 2020; Sievers and Nebelsick, 2018
Bird	Predation	Crushing	No	references in Kowalewski and Nebelsick, 2003
Turtles	Predation	Crushing	No	Chesher, 1969
Mammals	Predation	Crushing	No	Nebelsick, 1999
Crustaceans				
Predatory Decapods	Predation	Crushing	No	Nebelsick, 1999; Kowalewski and Nebelsick, 2003; Wisshak and Neumann, 2020
		Margin Damage	Yes	Merrill and Hobson, 1970; Weihe and Gray, 1968; Crozier, 1919; MacGinitie and MacGinitie, 1968
Shrimp	Commensal	None	No	Brasseur et al., 2018
Pea Crabs	Commensal or Parasitic	None	No	Campos-González, 1986; Campos and Griffith, 1990; Campos et al., 1992; Wirtz et al., 2009; Guilherme et al., 2015
Copepods	Parasitic	Test gall	Yes	Koehler, 1898; Bonnier, 1898; Solovyev, 1961; Boucot, 1990; Radwańska and Radwański, 2005; Radwańska and Poirot, 2010; Mehl et al., 1991
	Parasitic (?)	Spine gall	Yes	Stock, 1968; Radwańska and Radwański, 2005

Table 1 (cont.)

Predator/Symbiont	Interaction type	Trace producing	Fossil examples	Source
	Parasitic	None	No	Venmathi Maran et al., 2017; Humes, 1980; Dojiri and Humes,1982; Stock and Gooding, 1986
Barnacles	Parasitic (?)	Spine gall	No	Grignard and Jangoux, 1994; Grygier and Newman, 1991
	Parasitic or Commensal	Test gall	No	Grygier and Newman, 1991; Yamamori and Kato, 2020
	Commensal	Spine encrustation	Yes	pers. obs.
Echinoderms				
Asteroids	Predation	Crushing	No	Birkeland and Chia, 1971; Merrill and Hobson, 1970
Mollusks				
Cassid gastropod	Predation	*Oichnus*	Yes	Hughes and Hughes, 1971; Kowalewski and Nebelsick, 2003; Nebelsick et al., 1998; McClintock and Marion, 1993; Tyler et al., 2018; Grun et al., 2014; Farrar et al., 2020
Eulimid gastropod	Parasitic	*Oichnus*	Yes	see Table 2
		Spine gall	No	see Table 2
		Test gall	Yes	see Table 2
		None	No	see Table 2
Muricid gastropod	Parasitic	*Oichnus*	Yes	Vaïtilingon et al., 2004
Oyster	Commensal	Spine encrustation	Yes	Hopkins et al., 2004

Bryozoans				
Fenestellid	Commensal	Spine encrustation	Yes	Schneider, 2003
Cheilostomatid	Parasitic	Test encrustation	No	Queiroz, 2020
Annelids				
Hesionid polychaete	Commensal	None	Yes	Chim et al., 2013; Wisshak and Neumann, 2006
Serpulid polychaete	Commensal	Test encrustation	Yes	Wisshak and Neumann, 2006
		Spine encrustation	Yes	pers. obs.
Sponges				
Demosponge	Commensal	Spine encrustation	No	Cerrano et al., 2009; Hétérier et al., 2004
Brachiopod				
Rhynchonellid	Commensal	Spine encrustation	Yes	Schneider, 2003
Foraminifera				
Benthic foram	Parasitic	*Oichnus*	Yes	Neumann and Wisshak, 2006; Wisshak et al., 2023
Benthic foram	Commensal	Spine encrustation	No	Hopkins et al., 2004

prey upon echinoids (Kowalewski and Nebelsick, 2003). Turtles bite into the test and crush it to access the viscera, and Loggerhead turtles have been observed preying on the large spatangoid echinoid *Meoma ventricosa* (Chesher, 1969). Diverse predation strategies are used by birds, and these vary according to the bird species. Some peck holes in the tests whereas others carry the prey and drop it onto a hard surface to fracture the test. Sea otters are the most common marine mammals preying on echinoids, and they break the test, leaving no recognizable traces (Nebelsick, 1999).

Crustaceans and asteroids are common invertebrate predators of echinoids (Nebelsick, 1999). Spiny lobsters use their mandibles to crush the tests of small sea urchins, and they feed on larger individuals by piercing and opening the peristomal membrane to access the viscera. Some of the large spiny lobsters even consume small urchins entirely. For example, the lobster *Homarus americanus* has been observed cracking urchin tests into pieces and feeding on the viscera (Hagen and Mann, 1992). Spider crabs and rock crabs prey on regular and irregular echinoids. They pierce the peristomal membrane and enlarge the opening by removing pieces of the test and finally feed on the interior (Kowalewski and Nebelsick, 2003). The great spider crab *Hyas araneus* has been observed attacking the sea urchin *Strongylocentrotus* in the northern polar waters, and an individual was recorded surviving more than 40 hours after extensive test damage (Wisshak and Neumann, 2020). In sand dollars, crustaceans can leave behind marginal traces because of nonlethal predation (Zinsmeister, 1980; Nebelsick, 1999). Asteroids prey on echinoids, usually consuming the entire test (Merrill and Hobson, 1970; Birkeland and Chia, 1971). The sea urchin *Diadema antillarum* has been observed to prey on other echinoid species by removing their spines and creating a puncture hole in the test (Quinn, 1965), and echinoid spines have been found in the gut content of *Eucidaris tribuloides* (Serafy, 1979).

Whereas crushing predation by vertebrates has reduced probability of being recognized in the fossil record due to the near total destruction of the test, there have been a few instances where potential traces of this behavior have been identified. Neumann and Hampe (2018) interpreted a series of aligned circular puncture holes on the oral surface of a single specimen of the Maastrichtian holasteroid *Echinocorys ovata* as having been produced by a sublethal bite, potentially from a mosasauroid. Borszcz and Zatón (2013) described Jurassic fish regurgitates containing the disarticulated and etched plates and spines of cidaroids, representing some of the earliest direct evidence of fish predation on echinoids. Wilson et al. (2014) described slightly younger evidence of fish predation, from paired indentations on rhabdocidaroid echinoid spines that are interpreted as fish bite marks.

2.2 Margin Damage

Triggerfish prey on both regular and irregular echinoids (Frazer et al., 1991). When triggerfish attack regular urchins, they bite into the peristomal membrane and ingest the viscera (Kowalewski and Nebelsick, 2003). The gray triggerfish (*Balistes capriscus*) has been observed feeding on clypeasteroid echinoids in the Gulf of Mexico (Frazer et al., 1991; Kurz, 1995). The triggerfish uses a complex technique to capture and feed on its prey. It exposes the sand dollar with jets of water, after the test is exposed, it then grasps the sand dollar with its teeth, lifts it and drops it on the substrate until its oral side is facing upward. The fish will then attack by crushing the edges of the test with its jaws and feeding on the viscera. Successful attacks leave behind large wounds in the oral side, jagged wound edges, intraplate fragmentation, test abrasion, and parallel tooth marks on the test (Frazer et al., 1991; Kowalewski and Nebelsick, 2003). Cuspate-shaped bite marks on the ambitus produced in successful triggerfish attacks look similar to nonlethal marginal traces; however, they record lethal attacks and the damage is not limited to the ambitus. Similar traces have been observed in clypeasteroids in the Red Sea (Nebelsick, 2020 and references therein). Sublethal triggerfish attacks can be identified by apparent healing of the test along the damaged margin, though the irregular shape of the test outline persists in the surviving echinoid (Figure 1H and 1K). In this way, sublethal margin damage is akin to crab repair scars on mollusks and can be used as a proxy for unsuccessful predation.

Lethal or nonlethal test damage in clypeasteroid echinoids can be caused by both predation and hydrodynamics (Weihe and Grey, 1968; Lawrence and Tan, 2001 and references therein). Traces of nonlethal marginal test damage can be potentially diagnosed as biological in origin because of nonrandom species selectivity and site selectivity on tests. Marginal traces suggesting nonlethal predation have been observed on fossil and live specimens. This is not surprising given that clypeasteroids are robust and can survive multiple predatory attacks (Nebelsick et al., 1999). The prevalence of nonlethal predatory traces in the fossil record (Nebelsick et al., 1999) is attributed to the structural integrity of the test being preserved when the damage is limited to the ambitus (Nebelsick, 2020). Diverse predators that might produce nonlethal traces have been documented in Recent environments. These include predation by blue crabs (*Callinectes sapidus*) on *Mellita* (Weihe and Grey, 1968), *Cancer* sp. and sheep crabs (*Loxorhynchus grandis*) on *Dendraster excentricus* (Merrill and Hobson, 1970), benthic fish on *Leodia sexiesperforata* (Crozier, 1919), and spiny lobsters (*Panulirus interruptus)* on *Dendraster excentricus* (MacGinitie and MacGinitie, 1968). Nonlethal predatory traces are more common in large specimens, and it is suggested that damage to the ambitus in smaller individuals or juveniles might be

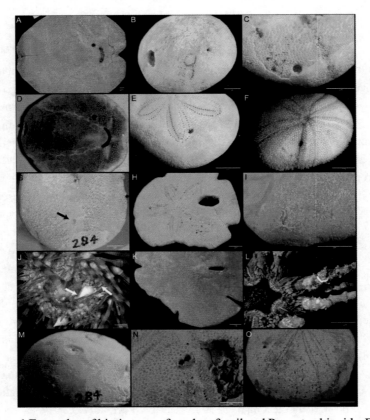

Figure 1 Examples of biotic traces found on fossil and Recent echinoids. Fossil (A–C) and Recent predation traces (D–F) produced from cassid gastropod predation. Note the highly beveled drill hole morphology in (A), and the subcircular drill hole morphology in (C). Parasitic trace on fossil echinoid (G) and Recent equivalent (J) denoted by arrows, with multiple eulimids still present on Recent specimen (also denoted by an arrow). Fossil (H) and modern (K) crab predation traces; fossil (I) and Recent (L) tube worm traces; fossil octopus predation trace (M); and post-depositional biotic traces with gastrochaenid bivalve borings (N) and clionid sponge borings (O). Species as follows: *Fernandezaster whisleri* (A, UF-IP 114520); *Rhyncholampas gouldii* (B, UF-IP 128804; C, UF-IP 5782; G, UF-IP 128439; M, UF-IP 128988); *Meoma ventricosa* (D, UF-IZ uncatalogued); *Clypeaster reticulatus* (E, UF-IZ 431); *Echinoneus cyclostomus* (F, UF-IZ 2642); *Encope tamiamiensis* (H, UF-IP 13759); *Oligopygus wetherbyi* (I, UF-IP 47955; O, UF-IP 46714); *Echinothrix calamaris* (J, UF-IZ 2226); *Encope michelini* (K, UF-IZ 4939); *Plococidaris verticillata* (L, UF-IZ 11109); *Clypeaster rosaceus* (N, UF-IZ 125419). Scale bars 1 cm

lethal (Lawrence and Tan, 2001). According to Crozier (1919), the presence of multiple bites on a single test may be due to the fragility of the ambitus of the test or its form, making it easier for predators to break off pieces. Test damage tends to be more frequent in the posterior side of clypeasteroid tests (Weihe and Gray, 1968; Borzone, 1992, 1994; Nebelsick and Kampfer, 1994; Sonnenholzner and Lawrence, 1998; Laurence and Tan, 2001). Higher exposure of the posterior region of the test when buried in the substrate might cause more frequent attacks on the posterior portion of the test (Crozier, 1919).

2.3 Drilling Predation

Cassid gastropods (family Cassidae) are well-known echinoid-targeting specialist predators today and produce diagnostic drill hole traces on their prey, which can be used to quantify the intensity of this biotic interaction in the fossil record

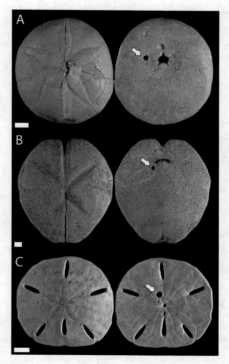

Figure 2 Examples of traces interpreted as predatory cassid drill holes in fossil and Recent echinoids. (A) Cassiduloid echinoid *Rhyncholampas evergladensis* from the Pliocene of Florida (UF-IP 21420). (B) Spatangoid echinoid *Fernandezaster whisleri* from the Pliocene of Florida (UF-IP 114520).
(C) Recent clypeasteroid echinoid *Leodia sexiesperforata* from the Bahamas (UF-IZ 18904). Arrows indicate drill holes. Adoral view left, oral view right. Scale bar 1 cm

(Hughes and Hughes, 1971; McNamara, 1994; Nebelsick et al., 1998; Kowalewski and Nebelsick, 2003; Figures 1A–F and 2). Predation pressure by cassids can be high, leading to considerable echinoid mortality with drilling frequencies of 95 percent in some Recent populations (McClintock and Marion, 1993; Tyler et al., 2018). In many respects, cassid drilling behavior on echinoids is mechanistically analogous to that of other gastropod predators, such as naticids and muricids on mollusks, in that they actively hunt their prey and use a combination of mechanical and chemical dissolution to weaken the skeletal structure and gain access to internal tissue (Hughes and Hughes, 1971). Though understudied with respect to mollusk-associated drill holes, the microstructure, morphology, and stereotypy of echinoid-associated drill holes has recently become the focus of renewed interest (e.g., Grun et al., 2014; Tyler et al., 2018; Farrar et al., 2020). Recent studies have additionally shown that the position of the drill hole relative to particular test structures (e.g., pore pairs, plate boundaries, tubercles) can dramatically alter the morphology of the drill hole (Złotnik and Ceranka, 2005a; see also discussions in Farrar et al., 2020). The resulting wider range of drill hole morphologies on echinoids relative to those found on mollusk prey have perhaps impeded wide-scale efforts quantifying drill hole occurrences to the same extent as have been done for mollusks (e.g., Kelley et al., 2003; but see Petsios et al., 2021). Though other forms of trace-producing predation are known to occur on Recent or fossil echinoids (e.g., Sievers et al., 2014; Wilson et al., 2014; Grun, 2016; Sievers and Nebelsick, 2018; see discussion above), drill holes remain the best proxy for consistent assessment of predation intensity across longer timescales.

3 Parasites and Other Symbionts

Parasitism is common in Recent ecosystems (Poulin, 2011; Leung, 2017) and is known to be a significant driver of co-evolutionary adaptive pressures in host and parasite species. The complex relationship between parasites and their potentially multiple hosts across different parasite life stages make unraveling the evolutionary history of this interaction difficult in most cases (De Baets and Littlewood, 2015). Studying parasitism in the fossil record at macroevolutionary scales is further obstructed by the paucity of fossilized evidence of parasitism, either in the form of the parasite body fossil itself, or a trace fossil of parasitic activities associated with the host (Donovan, 2015). Drilling, bioerosive, and gall-forming parasitism in Recent ecosystems which produce potentially diagnostic traces on echinoid hard parts (Jangoux, 1987), are among the most likely to be recognized in the fossil record and can give critical insights into the evolution of echinoid-targeting parasitism.

3.1 Parasites That Produce Holes

Oichnus-type circular to subcircular depressions or holes produced by echinoid parasites have been distinguished from drill holes produced by predators mostly based on their much smaller size but sometimes by the morphology of the trace (see discussions in Farrar et al., 2020). However, though some detailed descriptions exist of traces produced by a known parasite observed in direct contact with the echinoid host (see Warén and Crossland, 1991), few studies of Recent echinoids document or illustrate the style of attachment and the presence, absence and/or detailed morphology of drill holes at the attachment site beyond noting the association (see Warén, 1980b for examples). The diversity of drill hole trace morphologies produced by parasites is, thus, likely severely under-represented in the literature, hindering diagnosis of the ecology of these traces in the fossil record.

3.1.1 Eulimid Parasites

Ongoing efforts to clarify behaviors of trace-producing parasites focus on eulimid gastropods, the most common macroinvertebrate echinoid parasite (Warén, 1983; Figure 1J). Eulimid gastropods (family Eulimidae) are echinoderm specialized parasites (Pearse and Cameron, 1991) and are known to parasitize all five echinoderm classes: crinoids (Schiaparelli et al., 2007; Dgebuadze et al., 2012), asteroids (Elder, 1979; Janssen, 1985; Salazar and Reyes-Bonilla, 1998), holothurians (Will, 2009; González-Vallejo and Amador-Carrillo, 2021), ophiuroids (Warén, 1983; Dgebuadze et al., 2020), and echinoids (references in Table 1). Generally, eulimid genera are specific to hosts up to the level of order, though some occur on more distantly related hosts (e.g., the genus *Pelseneeria* occurs on cidaroids, diadematids, and camerodonts and the genus *Vitreolina* occurs on arbacioids, camerodonts, and diademids). Despite being one of the most diverse gastropod families with more than 100 genera and 1000 species (Takano and Kano, 2014; Marshall and Bouchet, 2015), the majority of species lack host information (Warén and Crossland, 1991) for various reasons related to the difficulty of collection, preservation, and systematic description of parasite-host association for zoological collections (e.g., Geiger, 2016).

Eulimid parasites can be either endo- or ectoparasitic, with some highly specialized endoparasitic forms having lost a calcified shell completely (Warén, 1983). Ectoparasitic eulimids generally retain caenogastropod homologies, although many lack a radula or the proboscis (Warén, 1983). Despite this, eulimids have been observed producing drill hole traces in echinoid hosts, likely through some method of stereom dissolution, although the specific mechanisms at play are not well understood (Warén and Crossland, 1991). The "snout" of ectoparasitic eulimids consists of the proboscis (if

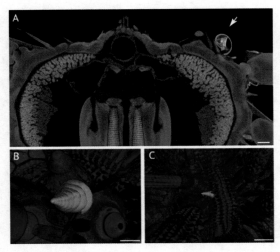

Figure 3 Micro-CT scans of two eulimid ectoparasites (Eulimidae indet., UF-IZ 463395) attached to *Plococidaris* sp. (UF-IZ 13593) at the (A–B) external interambulacral region of the echinoid host and (C) to the pore-pairs of the ambulacral region of the same echinoid. Scale bar 1 mm

present) and the specialized organ called the pseudopallium, which can be used to attach to the host and generally denudes the surrounding area of spines and may produce a circular pit scar. In Recent echinoids, ectoparasitic eulimids have been observed to attach to either the test (both in the interambulacral and ambulacral regions, Figure 3), peristomal membrane, periproct or periproctal membrane (including on the gonopores), and primary spines (Table 2). In the case of *Thyca*, female eulimids are known to use the pseudopallium to attach to hosts, which then aids the penetration of the proboscis through the exoskeleton, likely through chemical digestion of the stereom (Neumann and Wisshak, 2009 and references therein). This unique attachment strategy produces a relatively small, smooth-edged drill hole with an associated attachment halo trace, which had so far only been observed in asteroid-eulimid associations in present-day populations. Halo-bearing complete and incomplete drill hole traces in fossil echinoids have been postulated to represent a potentially extinct association of holasteroids and eulimids with similar attachment strategies observed in *Thyca* (Neumann and Wisshak, 2009). Eulimids associated with extant clypeasteroids can produce similarly small, circular, and smooth-edged drill hole traces lacking attachment haloes (Warén, 1981a). However, population surveys show that some eulimids attached to the test had penetrated the skeletal material (Crossland et al., 1991). Those that do penetrate the test where attached, specifically to the apical disk and petals, are presumably targeting the gonadal tissue (Crossland

Table 2 Eulimid parasites on echinoid and associated skeletal traces

Parasite	Host	Attachment location	Classification	Source
Arbacioids				
Vitreolina philippii	*Arbacia lixula*	Peristome	Non-trace producing	Rodríguez et al., 2001; Rinadli and Malacologico, 1994
Camerodonts				
Vitreolina philippii	*Sphaerechinus granularis*	Not determined	Not determined (presumed non-trace producing)	Rodríguez et al., 2001; Oliverio et al. 1994
Vitreobalcis holdsworthi	*Mespilia globulus*	Not determined	Not determined	Warén, 1981a
Pelseneeria brunnea	*Heliocidaris erythrogramma*	Periproct	Drill hole	Smith, 1990
Pelseneeria profunda	*Echinus affinis*	Test (tube feet and epithelium)	Non-trace producing	Barel and Kramers, 1977; Warén, 1981b
Pelseneeria media	*Echinus affinis*	Test	Non-trace producing	Koehler and Vaney, 1908
Pelseneeria subamericana	*Pseudechinus magellanicus*	Test	Drill hole (elliptical) and enlarged gonopore	Pastorino and Zelaya, 2001
Pelseneeria bountyensis	*Pseudechinus magellanicus*	Not determined	Not determined	Warén, 1981b
Curveulima devians	*Echinus esculentus*	Test	Non-trace producing	Pastorino and Zelaya, 2001
Pelseneeria stylifera	*Echinus esculentus*	Spines	Non-trace producing	Barel and Kramers, 1977
Monogamus minibulla	*Echinometra lucunter*	Test (general)	Pit scar and enlarged pore	González-Vallejo, 2008

Table 2 (cont.)

Parasite	Host	Attachment location	Classification	Source
Vitreobalcis sp.	*Salmacis bicolor*	Test (tube feet and epithelium)	Non-trace producing	Britayev et al., 2013; Ying, 2017
Vitreobalcis temnopleuricola	*Temnopleurus toreumaticus*	Apical disk/petals	Not determined	Fujioka, 1985
Vitreolina philippii	*Paracentrotus lividus*	Not determined	Not determined (presumed non-trace producing)	Rodríguez et al., 2001 Mifsud, 1990
Vitreolina philippii	*Psammechinus microtuberculatus*	Not determined	Not determined	Oliverio et al., 1994
Clypeasteroids				
Hypermastus tokunagai	*Scaphechinus mirabilis*	Test (general)	Pit scar (non-drilling)	Matsuda et al., 2008; Matsuda et al., 2010; Matsuda et al., 2013
Hypermastus placentae	*Arachnoides placenta*	Apical disk/petals	Drill hole	Crossland et al., 1991; Warén and Crossland, 1991; Crossland et al., 1993;
Turveria pallida	*Encope grandis*	Not determined	Not determined (presumed non-trace producing)	Warén and Crossland, 1991; Warén, 1992
Turveria pallida	*Encope* sp.	Not determined	Not determined	Warén, 1992
Turveria encopendema	*Encope* sp.	Not determined	Not determined	Warén and Crossland, 1991; Warén, 1992

Cidaroids

Species	Host	Attachment	Type	References
Nanobalcis nana	*Cidaris cidaris*	Primary spines	Not determined	Mifsud, 1990; Rodríguez et al., 2001
Nanobalcis worsfoldi	*Eucidaris tribuloides*	Primary spines	Non-trace producing	Warén and Mifsud, 1990; González-Vallejo and de León-González, 2018; Sales and Queiroz, 2021
Nanobalcis sp.	*Eucidaris thouarsii*	Not determined	Not determined	Warén, 1992
Nanobalcis cherbonnieri	*Prionocidaris baculosa annulifera*	Primary spines	Non-trace producing	Warén and Mifsud, 1990
Trochostilifer domus	*Stylocidaris* sp.	Primary spines	Gall-forming	Warén, 1980a; Warén, 1983
Trochostilifer eucidaricola *Vitreolina philippi.*	*Eucidaris tribuloides*	Peristome	Non-trace producing	Warén and Moolenbeek, 1989; Rodríguez et al., 2001
Pelseneeria sp.	*Eucidaris galapagensis*	Test and Primary Spines	Non-trace producing	Sonnenholzner and Molina, 2005
Sabinella bonifaciae	*Cidaris cidaris*	Test and Primary Spines	Spine thickening	Warén and Mifsud, 1990; Rodríguez et al., 2001
Sabinella troglodytes	*Eucidaris tribuloides*	Primary spines	Gall-forming	Thiele, 1925; Pilsbry, 1956; McPherson, 1968; Sarasúa and Espinosa, 1977; Warén, 1983; Queiroz et al., 2017; González-Vallejo and de León-González, 2018

Table 2 (cont.)

Parasite	Host	Attachment location	Classification	Source
Sabinella shaskyi	*Eucidaris thouarsii*	Primary spines	Gall-forming	Warén, 1992
Sabinella shaskyi	*Eucidaris galapagensis*	Primary spines	Gall-forming	Sonnenholzner and Molina, 2005
Sabinella infrapatula	*Ogmocidaris benhami*	Periproct	Drill hole	Warén, 1981b
Sabinella munita	*Goniocidaris tubaria*	Periproct	Drill hole	Warén, 1981a
Diadematids				
Fusceulima goodingi	*Centrostephoanus rodgersi*	Test (tube feet and epithelium)	Non-trace producing	Warén, 1981b
Pelseneeria hawaiiensis	*Aspidodiadema hawaiiensis*	Periproct	Enlarged gonopore	Warén, 1983;
				Pastorino and Zelaya, 2001
Echineulima leucophaes	*Diadema antillarum*	Test	Gall-forming	Philippi, 1845;
				Rodríguez et al., 2001
Microeulima sp.	*Chaetodiadema granulatum*	Not determined	Not determined	Warén, 1992
Vitreolina philippii	*Centrostephanus longispinus*	Not determined	Not determined	Oliverio et al., 1994
Spatangoids				
Haliella seisuimaruae	*Brissopsis* sp. cf. *luzonica*	Test	Pit scar (non-drilling)	Takano et al., 2020
Melanella alba	*Spatangus purpureus*	Not determined	Not determined	Barel and Kramers, 1977

et al., 1991, 1993). In the limited cases, where details of the parasite-host biology are known (e.g., Warén and Crossland, 1991; Crossland et al., 1991), the parasite remains on the host for a few days, after which the host quickly heals the site of attachment and/or penetration. Whether or not non-trace producing associations like these still produce a skeletal trace or indentations that would be identifiable and diagnostic in the fossil record is a matter of further study. Thus, there are numerous hurdles to diagnosing and cataloging probable eulimid drill hole traces in the fossil record.

Identification of trace fossils produced by eulimid parasitism is generally more challenging relative to cassid or fish predation. In the case of drilling eulimid parasitism, the drill hole may heal completely after the parasite abandons the host (Warén and Crossland, 1991) leaving no skeletal evidence of the association. Nevertheless, drill holes attributed to eulimid parasitism have been identified in the fossil record. Kier (1981) described multiple traces on the Early Cretaceous spatangoid *Hemiaster elegans washitae*. However, as pointed out by Warén (1991), these traces predate the first known fossil occurrence of the Eulimidae in the Late Cretaceous (Sohl, 1964). The largest trace, which exhibits similar characteristics to Recent eulimid traces that form pit scars at the attachment site, likely formed *syn-vivo* based on the deformed growth of the ambulacral plates in the affected petal (Kier, 1981). It is likely that a hitherto unknown eulimid or eulimid ancestor may be responsible for the trace considering the relatively short time gap (17 to 41 Ma) between the Albian occurrence of this trace and the Campanian appearance of eulimids. The absence of eulimids during this interval may be the result of their poor fossil record in general, owing to their small size, thin shells, and lack of distinct shell characteristics that hinder preservation, collection, and identification. Neumann and Wisshak (2009) described several traces from Paleocene holasteroids that exhibit both penetrating and non-penetrating circular traces with conspicuous halos, which they likened to the attachment and penetration strategy of the Recent eulimid *Thyca* on their asteroid hosts. In some cases, the pit or attachment halo are far larger than any such Recent eulimid trace, confounding their interpretation. Additional fossil examples include those described by Donovan et al. (2010), Donovan and Jagt (2013), and Donovan et al. (2018), which document several instances of non-penetrating pit scars on holasteroids from the Maastrichtian. In one case, a single specimen exhibited 170 pit scars that are assumed to have been formed *syn-vivo* (Donovan et al., 2018). Selectivity of the attachment sites near the ambulacra suggests that the trace maker was likely feeding on tissue associated with the tube feet. It is not clear that these traces were formed by eulimid parasites, but the non-penetrating pit scars and tube feet targeting behavior is known in Recent eulimids, though these behaviors are not known to occur simultaneously.

3.1.2 Muricid Parasites

A less common parasitic association involves the muricid gastropod *Vexilla vexillum*, which grazes on the epidermis of various echinoid hosts, including the echinometrid *Colobocentrotus* spp., and the camarodonts *Echinometra mathaei* and *Tripneustes gratilla*. Vaïtilingon et al. (2004) described the life cycle and recruitment of the parasite and the impact of their feeding on the echinoid hosts. In *T. gratilla*, they observed that on smaller lesions, tube feet, spines, and pedicellaria regenerated after the parasite was removed, and did not result in alteration to the skeletal test. Larger lesions, however, were subject to secondary infestation and deteriorated to the point where the test was perforated, resulting in a skeletal trace. These traces were subcircular to irregular in outline, penetrated completely through the test, and led to host mortality. Trace fossils resembling this type of lesion have been documented in fossil echinoids (Farrar et al., 2020).

3.1.3 Foraminifera Parasites

Foraminiferan parasitism has been postulated based on traces observed in fossils of the Maastrichtian holasteroid *Echinocorys perconica*. Neumann and Wisshak (2006) described shallow circular to subcircular indentations with an elevated rim on the outer margin of the oral side of the test, sometimes with a shallow central boss. These pits were thought to represent the outline of complete foraminifera tests, and the size and shape of these indentations has thus been used as a proxy for the size and shape of the parasite. Some pits have evidence of tubercle regeneration, indicating that this association was *syn-vivo*. The authors interpreted this interaction as similar to the modern-day behavior of the benthic foraminifera *Hyrrokkin sarcophaga* which is parasitic on shelly mollusks.

3.2 Parasites That Form Galls

Parasitic associations that result in the formation of a calcified gall on the test or spines of echinoids have been reported from Recent associations and less commonly from fossils.

3.2.1 Eulimid Galls

Some eulimid genera exhibit a unique parasitic strategy, whereby they form and occupy hollow gall domiciles on echinoid spines. The eulimid genera *Sabinella* and *Trochostilifer* form calcified galls on cidaroid spines in Recent ecosystems (McPherson, 1968; Warén, 1980a; Queiroz et al., 2017; González-Vallejo and

Figure 4 Eulimid spine galls on *Eucidaris*. (A) *Sabinella* eulimid gastropod galls on *Eucidaris tribuloides* spines (LACM E.1985–240.7), preserved attached (arrow) to test with eulimid parasite brood in the gall cavity. (B) Close-up of spine in A. (C) X-ray slice of spine gall cavity on *E. tribuloides* with eulimid parasite. (D) *Sabinella* eulimid gastropod galls on *Eucidaris thouarsii* (LACM E.1949–89.11) spines (arrow). (E) Close-up of spine in D. Scale bar 1 cm

de León-González, 2018). Spine galls have so far only been documented on cidaroids, which are especially vulnerable to epibiont attachment due to having exposed cortex without an epithelial layer in fully matured spines, unlike the spines of regular euechinoids (Ebert, 1986). The eulimid parasites are commonly found within the gall cavity, and it is not uncommon to find both the larger female, smaller male, and egg pouches preserved in association (Figure 4). Both female and male *Sabinella* have been observed to attach to the floor of the gall cavity with their snout, producing circular indentations in the gall material (González-Vallejo and de León-González, 2018). Eulimids found within fully formed galls exhibit fewer instances of shell breakage, suggesting that the gall serves as protection for the female-male pair (Warén, 1992).

The gall material itself is calcified but exhibits malformed stereom that is less dense than healthy spine stereom (Figure 4D). The exact growth mechanism is unclear, but it is thought that the continued presence of the parasite triggers abnormal cell proliferation and growth, similar to the formation of a tumor (Queiroz et al., 2017). In galls from the parasite *Sabinella*, the initial gall forms as a small depression at the site of attachment that gradually grows until a cavity is formed (Warén, 1992). Feeding by the eulimid continues to erode the spine material, likely by corrosive substances delivered via the proboscis at the site of

attachment (Queiroz et al., 2017). Although it has not been studied as exten-
sively it can be assumed that similar mechanisms are at play in galls formed by
the parasite *Trochostilifer.*

In the cases of eulimid-induced spine galls on cidaroids, the host may heal the
affected spine (Warén, 1992), or even potentially shed it (Prouho, 1887), though
the full life cycle of galled spines has not been thoroughly documented. If the
predominant method the host employs against galling parasites is to heal the
spine, then this would reduce the frequency of galled spines being preserved as
fossils. The opposite would apply if the hosts predominantly shed galled spines.
Nevertheless, the gall is comprised of skeletal material, though malformed, and
should have some likelihood of entering the fossil record. However, there are no
known examples of fossil galled spines to date, despite targeted efforts by the
authors. The present authors examined >700 cidaroid spines from Pliocene and
Recent populations from California and Florida for evidence of galls and other
symbiotic traces. In Florida, fossils of *Eucidaris tribuloides* are presumed to be
the likely ancestors of the living *E. tribuloides* populations in the eastern Gulf of
Mexico, as are the *E. thouarsii* fossil and Recent populations on the California
coast. Recent populations exhibited extensive fouling by bryozoans, annelids,
sponges, and barnacles, which has been documented previously (Hopkins et al.,
2004). Galled spines in various stages of development were also documented,
though these were less common than spines with epibionts. Male and female
specimens of *Sabinella* were present in some galls. Interestingly, spines with
galls had no other epibionts present on those spines, despite extensive fouling of
neighboring spines (Figure 4). In well-developed galls, the internal cavity was
found to be encroaching on or in some cases completely replacing the healthy
central medulla (core) of the spine, increasing the likelihood of breakage. No
evidence of galls was found in either the California or Florida Pliocene spines
examined. The Recent spines were more heavily fouled relative to their fossil
counterparts, and there was evidence of encrustation by epibionts on some fossil
spines (Figure 5), but this too was not as extensive as that in analogous Recent
populations. There is also no known fossil occurrence of *Sabinella* in Pliocene
assemblages in either region, suggesting that either the Pliocene echinoid
populations may not have been experiencing parasitism pressure by this eulimid, which was either rare or absent, or possibly poorly preserved due to
the small size and thin shell of *Sabinella*. This raises the possibility that the gall-
forming association with *Sabinella* may have recently evolved, or at least
recently intensified in both regions, possibly due to anthropogenic impacts.
Though parasitism intensity is generally thought to increase in anthropogenic-
ally impacted populations (e.g., Vidal-Martinez et al., 2010; Huntley et al.,
2014), Sonnenholzner et al. (2011) demonstrated that overfished food webs in

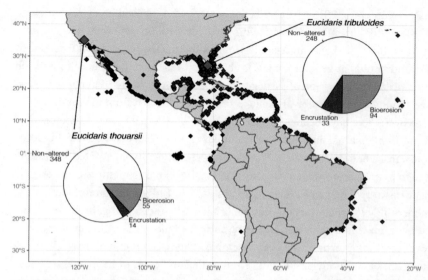

Figure 5 *Eucidaris tribuloides* and *Eucidaris thourarsii* distribution in North and South America. Large diamonds indicate Pliocene fossil spines surveyed for evidence of galling, while small diamonds indicate Recent occurrences as reported on GBIF.org. Pie charts show the number of Pliocene fossil spines that were non-altered, encrusted, or eroded. No galls were observed

the Galapagos region tend to have reduced eulimid density on echinoids, due to complex feedback between top predators, echinoid-targeting commensal crabs, and their eulimid prey. Alternatively, the preservation potential of galled spines may be severely reduced due to the gall compromising the structural integrity of the spine, both by causing the proliferation of malformed and less dense stereom, and by degrading the healthy spine core. In either case, additional exploration is needed to determine the likely cause of this discrepancy between fossil and Recent populations.

3.2.2 Copepod Galls

Gall-forming copepods are known to parasitize deep-sea echinothurioid echinoids. Anton et al. (2013) described the gall-forming behavior of *Pionodesmotes domhainfharraigeanus* on *Sperosoma grimaldii* and *Pionodesmotes phormosomae* on *Hygrosoma petersii*. Other authors described the internal cysts formed by the same copepod, *Pionodesmotes phormosomae*, on echinothurioid *Phormosoma uranus* (Bonnier, 1898; Koeler, 1898; Solovyey, 1961; Boucot, 1990). The galls in both cases are formed internally, in the ambulacral region of the test, indicating that the juvenile parasite uses the pore-pairs to gain entry to the test (Anton et al., 2013). The galls are comprised of skeletal material (Koehler, 1898), similar to galls associated with other parasites on echinoids. The combination of the galls being internal, as well as the relatively poor fossil record of echinothurioids in general, owing to their deep-sea habitat and thin, imbricated test, means that this type of association has a low probability of being preserved and found, and predictably, has not yet been documented from the fossil record. However, there have been numerous examples of external test cysts documented from fossil cidaroid and salenioid echinoids (Radwańska and Radwański, 2005; Radwańska and Poirot, 2010). These cysts were originally interpreted as forming due to trematode infestations by Mehl et al. (1991) but reinterpreted as copepod parasitism by Radwańska and Radwański (2005) given the similarities to the modern-day internal cysts on echinothurioids. These external galls are calcified, bulbous, and highly elevated above the surface of the test, and, depending on the level of development of the cyst, resemble "halloween pumpkin masks" (*sensu* Radwańska and Radwański, 2005). Imaged examples from Late Jurassic cidaroids *Plegiocidaris coronata*, *Plegiocidaris crucifera*, and *Plegiocidaris monilifera*, and the salenioids *Hemicidaris intermedia* and *Acrosalenia spinosa* depict an irregularly shaped bulbous mass, with irregularly spaced pores on the surface forming on the interambulacral region of the host (Mehl et al., 1991; Radwańska and Radwański, 2005; Radwańska and Poirot, 2010). This is likely an extinct parasite association, as these external copepod galls have not been documented from Recent echinoids.

Malformed spines have also been documented as the result of copepod parasitism in Recent echinothurioid echinoids. Stock (1968) described these galls as having the appearance of "bird nests glued against a stem," with the copepod inhabiting an asymmetrical swelling halfway up the spine. These galls have been documented in the echinothurioid *Calveriosoma gracile* and *Hygrosoma hoplacantha*, caused by copepods *Calvocheres globosus* and *Calvocheres engeli*, respectively (Stock, 1968). Simonelli (1889), and Radwańska and Radwański (2005) reported on similarly shaped cysts on a two cidaroid spines, one from the Jurassic and the other from the Miocene. The morphology of these cysts as described are unlike those documented from present-day eulimid domicile cysts, and so are tentatively described as copepod infestations, based on similarities to copepod-induced swelling on present-day echinothurioid spines and crinoid arm pinnules. These types of spine galls have yet to be documented in the fossil record on echinothurioids, which is unsurprising given the small and fragile nature of echinothurioid spines and their deep-sea habitat. Additionally, Stock (1968) described the gall material itself as calcified but loose, implying the malformed skeletal material of the affected spine is likely even more fragile still.

3.2.3 Barnacle Galls

Barnacles are common epizoans on echinoid hosts, typically benefiting from using the echinoid test or spines as a suitable substrate for settlement. A morphologically unique gall is formed on the test of the host during the symbiotic association of the stalked barnacle *Rugilepas pearsei* on the diadematids *Echinothrix diadema* and *Diadema setosum* (Grygier and Newman, 1991; Yamamori and Kato, 2020). On *Echinothrix diadema* the galls are described as semi-open, occurring in the interambulacral oral area of the outer surface of the host (Yamamori and Kato, 2020). In *Diadema setosum,* Grygier and Newman (1991) additionally described test scarring on the internal surface of the host's test as a result of gall formation. In life, the barnacle is camouflaged in the same color as the epidermis of the host and surrounded by the toxin-bearing secondary spines of the host. After death, the gall appears as a raised crater-shaped calcified gall that is distinct from the rounded galls formed by copepods. The walls and base of the gall are thickened, and the center pit of the gall has puncture holes where the peduncular attachment appendages of the barnacle are anchored deeply into the host. A single gall may be occupied by two to four mating barnacles, the number of which can be determined by the number of anchor holes. The barnacle is a suspension feeder and does not feed on the echinoid host's tissue, so this association is not clearly parasitic in nature (Grygier and Newman, 1991; Yamamori and Kato, 2020). Though galls were common in the populations studied by Yamamori and Kato (2020), with more than 9 percent of *E. diadema* individuals bearing galls, none have been described from the fossil record to date.

The pedunculate barnacle *Microlepas diademae*, on the other hand, is documented to attach not to the test but to the tips of primary spines of the host diademid *Echinothrix calamaris* (Grygier and Newman, 1991; Grignard and Jangoux, 1994). Infested spines are noticeably shorter than surrounding healthy primary spines. The infested spines are club-shaped rather than needle-shaped and, like the test galls, exhibit puncture holes from the peduncular attachment appendages of the barnacle. Grignard and Jangoux (1994) observed that infested spines were not able to regenerate or heal, even following the removal of the epibiont. This case of spine infestation is unique, as regular euechinoid spines are generally devoid of epibionts due to the epidermal layer that still surrounds fully grown spines, in contrast to cidaroids. To our knowledge, no diademid spines with clear barnacle infestation have been documented in the fossil record.

3.3 Encrusting and Bioerosive Associations

Encrusting epibionts are commonly present on both Recent and fossil echinoids (Zamora et al., 2008; Borszcz, 2012), with a number of these interactions occurring *syn-vivo*. As noted above, an association must exhibit demonstrable reduction in the fitness of the host to be deemed parasitic; and for many Recent and fossil echinoid-symbiont associations, detrimental effects on the host have not been demonstrated conclusively. These associations, whether parasitic, commensal, or mutualistic, are prevalent in Recent echinoids, though few are likely to be recognized in the fossil record, except in instances of exceptional preservation.

3.3.1 Boring Associations

A commensal relationship between a boring polydorid polychaete of the Maastrichtian holasteroid *Echinocorys ovata* was interpreted by Wisshak and Neumann (2006) from linear to sinuous traces on the oral side of the test on a single specimen. Evidence of test healing suggests that this association is *syn-vivo*. An echinoid-polydorid association like this is not known from Recent ecosystems, so the nature of this association is inferred indirectly based on the commensalism observed between Recent polydorid polychaetes and mollusks.

3.3.2 Spine Fouling

The most common form of encrustation in echinoids is via spine fouling by various groups of epibionts. A large diversity of fouling organisms attaches to living cidaroid urchin spines, including bryozoans, annelids, sponges, foraminifera, mollusks, and barnacles (Hopkins et al., 2004). Cidaroid spines serve as favorable habitats for settling sessile organisms, especially in deep-sea benthic environments where hardgrounds are scarce (Hétérier et al., 2008), increasing the local diversity where cidaroid echinoids are present. Cerrano et al. (2009) described the fouling behavior of demosponges *Homaxinella balfourensis*, *Isodictya erinacea*, *Iophon unicorne*, and *Haliclona (Rhizoniera) dancoi* on the cidaroid *Ctenocidaris perrieri*. Hétérier et al. (2004) compared symbionts between *Ctenocidaris spinosa* and *Rhynchocidaris triplopora* and found that the more rugous spines of *C. spinosa* support a higher diversity of epibionts, suggesting that spine microstructure in cidaroids is adaptive for encouraging fouling behaviors. The authors observed that the epibiont cohorts were taxonomically distinct between the two cidaroids, suggesting specialization on the part of the symbiont to specific species of hosts.

In the fossil record, direct evidence of spine encrustation is generally limited to biocalcifying organisms such as bryozoans, barnacles, and oysters, and is commonly present on fossil cidaroid echinoid spines. Less direct evidence of other types of encrusters, such as boring polychaetes, is usually preserved as evidence of bioerosion on the spines. In cases of exceptional preservation, uncommon epibionts are observed. Schneider (2003) described the association between the Paleozoic stem group echinoid *Archaeocidaris brownwoodensis* and the spiriferid brachiopod *Crurithyris planoconvexa* in addition to encrustation by fenestellid bryozoan fronds. It is interpreted as a commensal relationship, with the epibionts benefiting from protection offered by the large spines and the echinoids receiving minimal camouflaging benefit. Archaeocidarid spinosity may be an adaptation to support epibionts in this manner (Schneider, 2005), as in Recent cidaroid descendants (Hétérier et al., 2004).

3.3.3 Encrustation

A rare instance of encrustation directly onto the test of an echinoid was described by Queiroz (2020), who observed a bryozoan colony of *Schizoporella errata* growing on the test of the camarodont *Echinometra lucunter*. The site of attachment was relatively large and was denuded of primary spines, secondary spines, and tube feet. When the colony was removed, the author observed an inflammatory response in the host at the attachment site, suggesting that this was a detrimental association for the host and could potentially be classified as parasitism. The test material under the site of attachment was not damaged, and the epidermis healed in a few days following the encrusters' removal, indicating that this association did not produce a skeletal pathology on the host itself that could be identified in the fossil record. However, as the bryozoan is itself calcifying, there is potential to find fossil evidence of this association, as long as it can be distinguished from postmortem encrustation by bryozoans on the test of the echinoid.

4 Non-trace Producing Associations

Echinoid-associated biotic interactions that do not produce long-term pathologies on the skeletal material of the test or that induce traces on echinoid skeletal material that does not readily preserve in fossils are likely to be highly underestimated in the fossil record. Understanding the prevalence of so-called invisible interactions in present-day ecosystems is the first step for determining the degree to which these types of associations are underrepresented in the fossil record (see examples in Table 2).

Many present-day eulimid-echinoid associations can be classified as non-trace producing in this way, such as the parasitism by the eulimid *Trochostilifer eucidaricola* on the peristomal membrane of *Eucidaris tribuloides* (Warén and Moolenbeek, 1989), which is readily degraded post-mortem and rarely found in even otherwise articulated fossil cidaroids (Donovan and Gordon, 1993). González-Vallejo and de León-González (2018) described a short-term association between the eulimid parasite *Nanobalcis worsfoldi* and *Eucidaris tribuloides*, with the eulimid living around the base of the primary spines but not producing a spine gall like the co-occurring *Sabinella troglodytes*. Warén (1981b) described an association of *Fusceulima goodingi* on a diadematid echinoid that likely targeted tube-feet and epithelial tissue, while not producing skeletal traces on the echinoid. The eulimid *Pelseneeria hawaiiensis* penetrated the test of the echinoid host via the gonopore, which would be difficult to recognize in the fossil record unless special care is taken to look for enlargement of gonopores or pore pairs. The present authors additionally document an instance of a eulimid (indet.) parasitizing a specimen of *Plococidaris* sp. in both the ambulacral and interambulacral regions (Figure 3), with neither eulimid producing an identifiable trace. The smaller eulimid (Figure 3C) may, however, be accessing internal host tissue via the pore-pairs.

Copepods are common symbionts on Recent echinoids; and whereas parasitic associations can produce skeletal galling in some cases, the majority of cases are non-trace producing. Venmathi Maran et al. (2017) described a non-trace producing symbiotic association between the poecilostomatoid copepods *Mecomerinx ohtsukai* and *Clavisodalis toxopneusti* on the camarodont *Toxopneustes pileolus*. The copepod *Onychocheres alatus* lives among the spines of *Diadema antillarum* (Stock and Gooding, 1986). Several species of the copepod genus *Clavisodalis* are described as living in the esophagus and jaw apparatus of several regular euechinoid taxa (Humes, 1980; Dojiri and Humes, 1982). Whereas copepod-echinoid associations are numerous and common in Recent ecosystems, there is little hope of preserving evidence of these associations in the fossil record, outside of the handful of copepod genera that are known to produce galls.

Associations between the hesionid polychaete *Oxydromus* cf. *angustifrons* and the camarodont echinoids *Salmacis sphaeroides* and *Temnopleurus toreumaticus* are described by Chim et al. (2013) as commensal in nature. The polychaetes preferentially live near the peristomal membrane of the echinoid and do not appear to negatively impact the host. Unlike the probable polychaete association described by Wisshak and Neumann (2006) on fossil holasteroids, this association leaves no skeletal evidence of the host, and therefore cannot be directly studied in the fossil record.

Pea crabs (the brachyuran family Pinnotheridae) are obligatory symbionts of a wide range of host organisms including bivalves, crustaceans, echinoderms, polychaetes, tunicates, and fish (e.g., Schmitt, 1973; Powers, 1977; Williams, 1984; Takeda et al., 1997; Thoma et al., 2005, 2009; Ahyong and Ng, 2007).

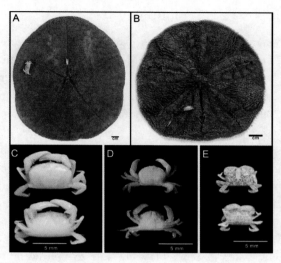

Figure 6 (A) *Clypeaster subdepressus*, infested by different crab species; *Dissodactylus latus* on the left and *Clypeasterophilus stebbingi* near the center. (B) *Mellita tenuis* infested by *Dissodactylus mellitae* from the Gulf of Mexico. Scale bar of echinoids = 1 cm. A closer look towards some commensal pea crabs (C) *D. latus,* (D) *C. stebbingi,* and (E) *D. mellitae.* Scale bar of crabs = 5 mm

Echinoids are frequently infested by pea crabs (Figure 6), which utilize their host to seek shelter, food, and a protected habitat for reproduction (e.g., Wirtz et al., 2009; Wirtz and Grave, 2009). Interactions between crabs and their echinoid hosts have been interpreted as either "commensal" or "parasitic" (e.g., Campos-González, 1986; Campos and Griffith, 1990; Campos et al., 1992; Wirtz and Grave, 2009; Guilherme et al., 2015). In the commensal interpretation, pea crabs do not harm the host but only feed on its fecal matter (Glassell, 1935). In contrast, according to the parasitic interpretation, crabs reduce host fecundity (De Bruyn et al., 2009) and feed on host tissues (e.g., Dexter, 1977; Telford, 1982; De Bruyn et al., 2009; Martinelli Filho et al., 2014). Interestingly, pea crabs appear to also be also able to prey on eulimid snails (Sonnenholzner et al., 2011) parasitizing their common host, suggesting that the infesting crabs may, at least occasionally, benefit their host. Regardless of the ecological interpretation of pinnerid–echinoid interactions, pea crab infestation is not known to result in any test or spine deformities or damage suggesting that symbiotic interactions with pea crabs are unlikely to be identifiable in the fossil record. However, to our knowledge, the ichnological consequences of pea crab infestation has not been investigated rigorously.

5 Evolutionary Trends

Predation pressure is thought to have played a significant role in echinoid evolution and may have led to the mid-Mesozoic infaunalization of echinoids (Kier, 1982), which coincides with the diversification of several important groups of predators during the Mesozoic Marine Revolution (Figure 7) (McRoberts, 2001). Infaunalization, therefore, may have been an evolutionary adaptation to escape increasing predation pressure (Kier, 1982). Although the infaunalization of irregular echinoids began during the Mesozoic Marine Revolution, their early morphology restricted burrowing to coarse grained sediments (Smith, 1984; Table 3). During the Early Jurassic, the infaunal life-mode was facilitated by the evolution of uniformly sized dorsal spines packed more densely together (Smith, 1984), which prevented suffocation in tightly packed sediment by creating a layer of water around the test (Smith, 1984). By the Eocene, clypeasteroid echinoids were able to burrow into fine-grained sediments (Smith, 1984). The globular shapes of some spatangoid tests may help support burrow walls preventing collapse, thus facilitating deep burrowing (Kanazawa, 1992). In contrast, the flattened test shapes are associated with shallow burrowing (Kanazawa, 1992), and may prevent the test from being disturbed by currents, and allow the test to be covered with sediment, acting as camouflage (Kier, 1974). The following morphological features are thought to be indicative of burrowing by various spatangoids and holasteroids (Smith, 1984): (1) the dense development of aboral tubercules that indicate aboral spines that prevented sediment from falling between the spines; (2) larger oval ambulacral pores in the adapical region of ambulacrum III versus ambital ambulacral pores that suggests the presence of tunnel-building tube feet; (3) sunken anterior ambulacrum with enlarged interambulacral tubercles adjacent that are used for constructing shafts; and (4) ambulacral pores that are larger than the adjacent tube-feet pores, indicating the presence of tunnel-building tube feet.

Irregular echinoids diversified rapidly during the Jurassic and Cretaceous, outpacing the diversity of "regular" echinoids by the Cretaceous (Figure 7). Drill holes, as proxies for predation pressure by cassid gastropods, increased in intensity much later in the Eocene (Petsios et al., 2021), suggesting that the evolutionary adaptations associated with infaunalization were likely not driven by cassid predation pressure, or at least not initially. Although the frequency of drill hole traces in mollusks has been classically used as a proxy for predation pressure (see discussion in Harper, 2016), in the case of echinoids, drilling predators may be less impactful on their prey's population dynamics than other forms of predation, such as crushing from actinopterygian fish, crustaceans, and

Table 3 Evolutionary history of echinoid infaunalization (Smith 1984)

Time period	Group	Morphology/life mode	Interpretation
Eocene	Clypeasteroids	Tiny but dense aboral spines, flattened test Infaunal, fine sands	Increased camouflage by covering flat test with sand (Kier, 1974)
Cretaceous	Holasteroids and spatangoids	Tunnel-building tube feet, dorsal fascioles, and dense spatulate aboral spines Infaunal, fine sediment	Fascioles developed to create a mucus gland to protect the test from sediment and to draw water in the burrow (Smith, 1984)
Middle Jurassic	Echinaceans	Additional and stronger oral tube feet, well developed phyllodes Shallow turbulent habitats	Phyllodes allowed for stronger attachments in turbulent environments (Kier, 1974)
Early Jurassic	Holectypygoids and galeropygoids	Denser dorsal spines Infaunal, coarse sediment	Smaller spines allowed the test to be covered with sediment for camouflage (Kier, 1974)
	Irregular echinoids (pygasteroids)	Epifaunal	Not adapted for borrowing (Smith, 1984)
Triassic	All regular echinoids	Protected habitats, deeper waters	Began to diversify for different habitats (Smith, 1984)
Paleozoic	All regular echinoids	Epifaunal Epifaunal Firm substrate, offshore or protected habitats	Regular echinoids do not have the morphology for successful burrowing (Kier, 1974)

Elements of Paleontology

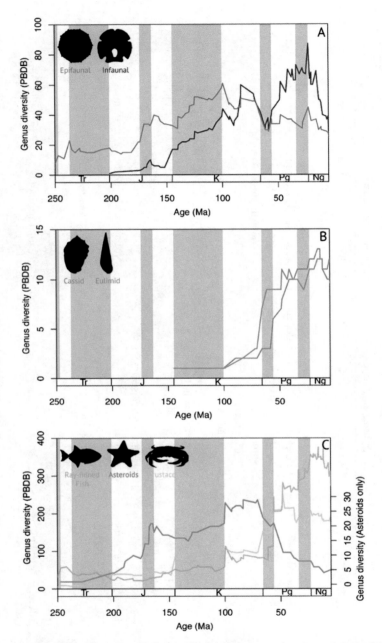

Figure 7 Mesozoic to Cenozoic trends in richness at the genus level of (A)
epifaunal and infaunal echinoids, (B) echinoid-targeting drilling gastropods,
and (C) crushing predators, as calculated from Paleontological Database
occurrences. Credit for organism silhouettes: PhyloPic (www.phylopic.org)

asteroids. Asteroids in particular experience rapid diversification earlier in the Mesozoic compared to fish and crustacean predators, suggesting that asteroid predation pressure may have played a role in the evolution of early infaunal echinoids (Figure 7). Nevertheless, estimating the intensity of crushing predation pressure in fossil communities remains challenging due to the difficulty of differentiating damage due to crushing versus abiotic or post-mortem breakage. Other methods, such as comparing temporal trends in taxonomic diversification and morphological change in predator and prey groups, can be employed instead.

6 Concluding Remarks

In modern oceans, the numerous biotic interactions that involve echinoids impact the fitness of individuals and health of echinoid communities. Such interactions undoubtedly impacted past populations as well; but without rigorous quantitative estimates of the intensity and frequency of biotic interactions in ancient ecosystems, we are unable to constrain to what extent these interactions have driven long-term ecological and evolutionary trends. Understanding the ecologies of the various biotic interactions which result in skeletal pathologies in living echinoids is key to successfully characterizing the numerous traces observed in fossil echinoids. As summarized here, a great diversity of predatory, parasitic, commensal, and mutualistic interactions is known from Recent ecosystems. Many of those interactions result in traces on echinoid skeletons that have been or have the potential to be successfully diagnosed in the fossil record. However, trace producing interactions are only a fraction of the total likely ecological associations impacting short term fitness and long-term adaptive evolution of echinoids. In such cases, indirect methods can be often employed to assess the roles of these invisible interactions. Taken together, these direct and indirect lines of evidence for the presence of biotic interactions involving echinoids can inform observed morphological, behavioral, and adaptive trends and quantify more rigorously ecological pressures in the evolutionary history of echinoids.

References

Aberhan, M., Kiessling, W., & Fürsich, F. T. (2006). Testing the role of biological interactions in the evolution of mid-Mesozoic marine benthic ecosystems. *Paleobiology*, *32*(2), 259–277.

Ahyong, S. T., & Ng, P. K. (2007). The pinnotherid type material of Semper (1880), Nauck (1880) and Bürger (1895) (Crustacea: Decapoda: Brachyura). *Raffles Bulletin of Zoology, Supplement*, *16*, 191–226.

Alekseev, A., & Endelman, L. (1989). Association of ectoparasitic gastropods with Upper Cretaceous echinoid *Galerites*. In Kaljo D. L., ed., *Fossil and Recent Echinoderm Researches*. Tallin: Academy of Sciences of the Estonian SSR, pp. 165–174.

Anton, R. F., Stevenson, A., & Schwabe, E. (2013). Description of a new abyssal copepod associated with the echinoid *Sperosoma grimaldii* Koehler, 1897. *Spixiana*, *36*, 201–210.

Barel, C. D. N., & Kramers, P. G. N. (1977). A survey of the echinoderm associates of the north-east Atlantic area. *Zoologische Verhandelingen*, 156 (1), 1–159.

Birkeland, C., & Chia, F.-S. (1971). Recruitment risk, growth, age and predation in two populations of sand dollars, *Dendraster excentricus* (Eschscholtz). *Journal of Experimental Marine Biology and Ecology*, *6*(3), 265–278.

Bonnier, J. (1898). *Note sur le Pionodesmotes phormosomae, copépode parasite du Phormosoma uranus*. In Albert I, Guerne, J. de, Richard, J., eds., Resultats des Campagnes Scientifiques accomplies sur son Yacht par Albert Ier, Prince souverain de Monaco, 12, 61–66, 10.

Borszcz, T. (2012). Echinoids as substrates for encrustation: Review and quantitative analysis. *Annales Societatis Geologorum Poloniae*, *82*(2), 139–149.

Borszcz, T., & Zatoń, M. (2013). The oldest record of predation on echinoids: Evidence from the Middle Jurassic of Poland. *Lethaia*, *46*(2), 141–145.

Borzone, C. (1992). El ciclo gonadal de *Venus antiqua* King & Broderip 1835 (Veneridae: Bivalvia) en el Golfo San Jose. *Physis*, *47*(113), 61–72.

Borzone, C. A. (1994). Distribución de la malacofauna en el infralitoral de una playa arenosa expuesta del sur del Brasil. *Revista de Investigaciones Científicas*, *5*, 23–26.

Boucot, A. J. (1990). *Evolutionary Paleobiology of Behavior and Coevolution*. Amsterdam: Elsevier, p. 725.

Brasseur, L., Caulier, G., Lepoint, G., Gerbaux, P., & Eeckhaut, I. (2018). *Echinometra mathaei* and its ectocommensal shrimps: The role of sea urchin spinochrome pigments in the symbiotic association. *Scientific Reports*, *8*(1), 1–10.

Britayev, T. A., Bratova, O., & Dgebuadze, P. Y. (2013). Symbiotic assemblage associated with the tropical sea urchin, *Salmacis bicolor* (Echinoidea: Temnopleuridae) in the An Thoi Archipelago, Vietnam. *Symbiosis*, *61*(3), 155–161.

Buatois, L. A., Mángano, M. G., Desai, B. et al. (2022). Infaunalization and resource partitioning during the Mesozoic Marine Revolution. *Geology*, *50*, 789–790.

Campos, E., & Griffith, H. (1990). *Clypeasterophilus*, a new genus to receive the small-palped species of the *Dissodactylus* complex (Brachyura: Pinnotheridae). *Journal of Crustacean Biology*, *10*(3), 550–553.

Campos, E., de Campos, A., & Ramirez, J. (1992). Remarks on distribution and hosts for symbiotic crustaceans of the Mexican Pacific (Decapoda and Isopoda). *Proceedings of the Biological Society of Washington*, *105*(4), 753–759.

Campos-González, E. (1986). Records and new host of pea crabs (Decapoda: Pinnotheridae) for Baja California, Mexico. *The Veliger*, *29*(2), 238–239.

Ceranka, T., & Zlotnik, M. (2003). Traces of cassid snails predation upon the echinoids from the middle Miocene of Poland. *Acta Palaeontologica Polonica*, *48*(3), 491–496.

Cerrano, C., Bertolino, M., Valisano, L., Bavestrello, G., & Calcinai, B. (2009). Epibiotic demosponges on the Antarctic scallop *Adamussium colbecki* (Smith, 1902) and the cidaroid urchins *Ctenocidaris perrieri* Koehler, 1912 in the nearshore habitats of the Victoria Land, Ross Sea, Antarctica. *Polar Biology*, *32*(7), 1067–1076.

Chesher, R. H. (1969). Contributions to the biology of *Meoma ventricosa* (Echinoidea: Spatangoida). *Bulletin of Marine Science*, *19*(1), 72–110.

Chim, C. K., Ong, J. J. L., & Tan, K. S. (2013). An association between a hesionid polychaete and temnopleurid echinoids from Singapore. *Cahiers de Biologie Marine*, *54*, 577–585.

Cross, N. E., & Rose, E. P. (1994). Predation of the Upper Cretaceous spatangoid echinoid *Micraster*. In Bruno D., Guille, A., Feral, J.-P., eds., *Echinoderms through Time*. CRC Press. London: Taylor & Francis, pp. 607–612.

Crossland, M., Alford, R. A., & Collins, J. (1991). Population dynamics of an ectoparasitic gastropod, *Hypermastus* sp. (Eulimidae), on the sand dollar, *Arachnoides placenta* (Echinoidea). *Marine and Freshwater Research*, *42*(1), 69–76.

Crossland, M., Collins, J., & Alford, R. (1993). Host selection and distribution of *Hypermastus placentae* (Eulimidae), and ectoparasitic gastropod on the sand dollar *Arachnoides placenta* (Echinoidea). *Marine and Freshwater Research, 44*(6), 835–844.

Crozier, W. J. (1919). On regeneration and the re-formation of lunules in *Mellita. The American Naturalist, 53*(624), 93–96.

De Baets, K., & Littlewood, D. T. J. (2015). The importance of fossils in understanding the evolution of parasites and their vectors. *Advances in Parasitology, 90*, 1–51.

De Bruyn, C., Rigaud, T., David, B., & De Ridder, C. (2009). Symbiosis between the pea crab *Dissodactylus primitivus* and its echinoid host *Meoma ventricosa*: Potential consequences for the crab mating system. *Marine Ecology Progress Series, 375*, 173–183.

Dexter, D. M. (1977). A natural history of the sand dollar *Encope stokesi* L. Agassiz in Panama. *Bulletin of Marine Science, 27*(3), 544–551.

Dgebuadze, P. Y., Fedosov, A. E., & Kantor, Y. I. (2012). Host specificity of parasitic gastropods of the genus *Annulobalcis* Habe, 1965 (Mollusca, Gastropoda, Eulimidae) from crinoids in Vietnam, with descriptions of four new species. *Zoosystema, 34*(1), 139–155.

Dgebuadze, P. Y., Mekhova, E. S., Thanh, N. T., & Zalota, A. K. (2020). Diet relationships between parasitic gastropods *Echineulima mittrei* (Gastropoda: Eulimidae) and sea urchin *Diadema setosum* (Echinoidea: Diadematidae) hosts. *Marine Biology, 167*(10), 1–4.

Dojiri, M., & Humes, A. (1982). Copepods (Poecilostomatoida: Taeniacanthidae) from sea urchins (Echinoidea) in the southwest Pacific. *Zoological Journal of the Linnean Society, 74*(4), 381–436.

Donovan, S. K. (2015). A prejudiced review of ancient parasites and their host echinoderms: CSI Fossil Record or just an excuse for speculation? *Advances in Parasitology, 90*, 291–328.

Donovan, S. K., & Gordon, C. M. (1993). Echinoid taphonomy and the fossil record: Supporting evidence from the Plio-Pleistocene of the Caribbean. *Palaios, 8*(3), 304–306.

Donovan, S. K., & Jagt, J. W. (2013). *Rogerella* isp. infesting the pore pairs of *Hemipneustes striatoradiatus* (Leske) (Echinoidea: Upper Cretaceous, Belgium). *Ichnos, 20*(4), 153–156.

Donovan, S. K., Jagt, J. W., & Dols, P. (2010). Ichnology of Late Cretaceous echinoids from the Maastrichtian type area (The Netherlands, Belgium)–2. A pentagonal attachment scar on *Echinocorys* gr. *conoidea* (Goldfuss). *Bulletin of the Mizunami Fossil Museum, 36*, 51–53.

Donovan, S. K., Jagt, J. W., & Langeveld, M. (2018). A dense infestation of round pits in the irregular echinoid *Hemipneustes striatoradiatus* (Leske) from the Maastrichtian of the Netherlands. *Ichnos, 25*(1), 25–29.

Donovan, S. K., Jagt, J. W., & Nieuwenhuis, E. (2016). Site selectivity of the boring *Rogerella* isp. infesting *Cardiaster granulosus* (Goldfuss) (Echinoidea) in the type Maastrichtian (Upper Cretaceous, Belgium). *Geological Journal, 51*(5), 789–793.

Ebert, T. A. (1986). A new theory to explain the origin of growth lines in sea urchin spines. *Marine Ecology Progress Series, 34,* 197–199.

Elder, H. Y. (1979). Studies on the host parasite relationship between the parasitic prosobranch *Thyca crystallina* and the asteroid starfish *Linckia laevigata. Journal of Zoology, 187*(3), 369–391.

Farrar, L., Graves, E., Petsios, E. et al. (2020). Characterization of traces of predation and parasitism on fossil echinoids. *Palaios, 35*(5), 215–227.

Frazer, T. K., Lindberg, W. J., & Stanton, G. R. (1991). Predation on sand dollars by gray triggerfish, *Balistes capriscus*, in the northeastern Gulf of Mexico. *Bulletin of Marine Science, 48*(1), 159–164.

Fujioka, Y. (1985). Population ecological aspects of the eulimid gastropod *Vitreobalcis temnopleuricola. Malacologia, 26*(1–2), 153–163.

Geiger, D. L. (2016). *Severnsia strombeulima* n. gen. & sp. from Hawaii (Mollusca, Gastropoda: Caenogastropoda: Eulimidae). *Zootaxa, 4084*(4), 587–589.

Gladfelter, W. (1978). General ecology of the cassiduloid urchin *Cassidulus caribbearum. Marine Biology, 47*(2), 149–160.

Glassell, S. A. (1935). New or little known crabs from the Pacific coast of northern Mexico. *Transactions of the San Diego Society of Natural History,* 8 (14), 163–180.

Gonzalez-Vallejo, N. E. (2008). Parasitism of Monogamus minibulla (Olsson and McGinty, 1958) (Gastropoda: Eulimidae) on the Red Sea-urchin Echinometra lucunter (Linnaeus, 1758)(Echinodermata: Echinometridae) on the Caribbean coast of Mexico. *Nautilus, 122*(3), 178.

González-Vallejo, N. E., & Amador-Carrillo, S. (2021). Assessment of *Megadenus holothuricola* Rosén, 1910 (Eulimidae), an endoparasite of *Holothuria mexicana* Ludwig, 1875 (Holothuriidae) in the southern Gulf of Mexico and the description a new species. *ZooKeys, 1016,* 49–61.

González-Vallejo, N. E., & León-González, J. Á. d. (2018). New ecological and taxonomic remarks on *Sabinella troglodytes* and *Nanobalcis worsfoldi* (Gastropoda: Eulimidae) living on the "slate-pencil sea urchin" from the Mexican Caribbean region. *Revista Mexicana de Biodiversidad, 89*(1), 123–133.

Grignard, J., & Jangoux, M. (1994). Occurrence and effects of symbiotic pedunculate barnacles on echinoid hosts. In David, B., Guille, A., Féral, J.-P., & Roux, M., eds., *Echinoderms through Time*. Rotterdam: Balkema, pp. 679–683.

Grun, T. B. (2016). Echinoid test damage by a stingray predator. *Lethaia*, *49*(3), 285–286.

Grun, T., Sievers, D., & Nebelsick, J. H. (2014). Drilling predation on the clypeasteroid echinoid *Echinocyamus pusillus* from the Mediterranean Sea (Giglio, Italy). *Historical Biology*, *26*(6), 745–757.

Grygier, M., & Neumann, W. A. (1991). A new genus and two new species of Microlepadidae (Cirripedia: Pedunculata) found on western Pacific diadematid echinoids. *Galaxea*, *10*(1), 1–22.

Guilherme, P. D., Brustolin, M. C., & Bueno, M. d. L. (2015). Distribution patterns of ectosymbiont crabs and their sand dollar hosts in a subtropical estuarine sandflat. *Revista de Biología Tropical*, *63*, 209–220.

Hagen, N. T., & Mann, K. (1992). Functional response of the predators American lobster *Homarus americanus* (Milne-Edwards) and Atlantic wolf-fish *Anarhichas lupus* (L.) to increasing numbers of the green sea urchin *Strongylocentrotus droebachiensis* (Müller). *Journal of Experimental Marine Biology and Ecology*, *159*(1), 89–112.

Harper, E. M. (2016). Uncovering the holes and cracks: From anecdote to testable hypotheses in predation studies. *Palaeontology*, *59*(5), 597–609.

Harper, E. M. (2022). Hunting evidence for the Mesozoic Marine Revolution: Progress and challenges. *Bollettino della Società Paleontologica Italiana*, *61*(1), 1–18.

Harper, E. M., & Skelton, P. (1993). The Mesozoic marine revolution and epifaunal bivalves. *Scripta Geologica, Special Issue*, *2*, 127–153.

Hautmann, M. (2004). Early Mesozoic evolution of alivincular bivalve ligaments and its implications for the timing of the "Mesozoic Marine Revolution." *Lethaia*, *37*(2), 165–172.

Hendler, G. (1977). The differential effects of seasonal stress and predation on the stability of reef-flat echinoid populations. *Proceedings of the Third International Coral Reef Symposium*, *1*, 217–223.

Hendler, G., Miller, J. E., Pawson, D. L., & Kier, P. M. (1995). *Sea Stars, Sea Urchins, and Allies: Echinoderms of Florida and the Caribbean*. Washington, DC: Smithsonian Institution Press. p. 390.

Hétérier, V., David, B., De Ridder, C., & Rigaud, T. (2008). Ectosymbiosis is a critical factor in the local benthic biodiversity of the Antarctic deep sea. *Marine Ecology Progress Series*, *364*, 67–76.

Hétérier, V., De Ridder, C., David, B., & Rigaud, T. (2004). Comparative biodiversity of ectosymbionts in two Antarctic cidarid echinoids, *Ctenocidaris spinosa* and *Rhynchocidaris triplopora*. *Echinoderms*. In Heinzeller, T., & Nebelsick, J., eds., *Proceedings 11th IEC, München*. London: Taylor & Francis, pp. 201–205.

Hopkins, T., Thompson, L., Walker, J., & Davis, M. (2004). A study of epibiont distribution on the spines of the cidaroid sea urchin, *Eucidaris tribuloides* (Lamarck, 1816) from the shallow shelf of the eastern Gulf of Mexico. In Heinzeller, T., & Nebelsick, J., eds., *Echinoderms München*. London: Taylor & Francis, pp. 207–211.

Hughes, R. (1981). Morphological and behavioural aspects of feeding in the Cassidae (Tonnacea, Mesogastropoda). *Malacologia, 20*, 385–402.

Hughes, R. N., & Hughes, H. P. (1971). A study of the gastropod *Cassis tuberosa* (L.) preying upon sea urchins. *Journal of Experimental Marine Biology and Ecology, 7*(3), 305–314.

Humes, A. G. (1980). A review of the copepods associated with holothurians, including new species from the Indo-Pacific. *Beaufortia, 30*(4), 31–123.

Huntley, J. W., Fürsich, F. T., Alberti, M., Hethke, M., & Liu, C. (2014). A complete Holocene record of trematode–bivalve infection and implications for the response of parasitism to climate change. *Proceedings of the National Academy of Sciences, 111*(51), 18150–18155.

Jangoux, M. (1987). Diseases of Echinodermata. 111. Agents metazoans (Annelida to Pisces). *Diseases of Aquatic Organisms, 3*, 59–83.

Janssen, H. H. (1985). Three epizoic gastropods from Malaysia and the Philippines. *Zeitschrift für Parasitenkunde, 71*(4), 553–560.

Kanazawa, K. I. (1992). Adaptation of test shape for burrowing and locomotion in spatangoid echinoids. *Palaeontology, 35*(4), 733–750.

Kelley, P. H., & Hansen, T. A. (2003). The fossil record of drilling predation on bivalves and gastropods. In Kelley, P. H., Kowalewski, M., & Hansen, T. A., ed., *Predator–Prey Interactions in the Fossil Record*. Boston: Springer, p. 20, pp. 113–139.

Kier, P. M. (1974). Evolutionary trends and their functional significance in the post-Paleozoic echinoids. *Paleontological Society Memoir 5. Journal of Paleontology, 48 (Suppl. to No. 3)*, 1–95.

Kier, P. M. (1981). A bored Cretaceous echinoid. *Journal of Paleontology, 55*(3), 656–659.

Kier, P. M. (1982). Rapid evolution in echinoids. *Palaeontology, 25*(1), 1–9.

Klompmaker, A. A., Kelley, P. H., Chattopadhyay, D. et al. (2019). Predation in the marine fossil record: Studies, data, recognition, environmental factors, and behavior. *Earth-Science Reviews, 194*, 472–520.

Koehler, R. (1898). *Echinides et ophiures provenant des campagnes du yacht l'Hirondelle:(Golfe de Gascogne, Açores, Terre Neuve)*. London: Imprimerie de Monaco. 12, pp. 1–78.

Kœhler, R., & Vaney, C. (1908). *Account of the Littoral Holothurioidea Collected by the Royal Indian Marine Survey Ship Investigator.* Calcutta: Order of the trustees of the Indian Museum. 3, pp. 1–54.

Kowalewski, M., & Nebelsick, J. H. (2003). Predation on recent and fossil echinoids. In *Predator – Prey Interactions in the Fossil Record, Vol. 20.* Boston: Springer, pp. 279–302.

Kowalewski, M., Dulai, A., & Fursich, F. T. (1998). A fossil record full of holes: The Phanerozoic history of drilling predation. *Geology, 26*(12), 1091–1094.

Kurz, R. C. (1995). Predator-prey interactions between gray triggerfish (*Balistes capriscus* Gmelin) and a guild of sand dollars around artificial reefs in the northeastern Gulf of Mexico. *Bulletin of Marine Science, 56*(1), 150–160.

Lawrence, J. M., & Tan, C.-Y. (2001). Test damage to the sand dollar *Mellita tenuis* on the Florida Gulf Coast. *Gulf of Mexico Science, 19*(1), 50–54.

Leung, T. L. (2017). Fossils of parasites: What can the fossil record tell us about the evolution of parasitism? *Biological Reviews, 92*(1), 410–430.

Levitan, D. R., & Genovese, S. J. (1989). Substratum-dependent predator-prey dynamics: Patch reefs as refuges from gastropod predation. *Journal of Experimental Marine Biology and Ecology, 130*(2), 111–118.

MacGinitie, G. E., & MacGinitie, N. (1968). *Natural History of Marine Animals.* 2nd ed. New York: McGraw-Hill Book Company, p. 523.

Madsen, F., & Wolff, T. (1965). Evidence of the occurrence of *Ascothoracica* (parasitic cirripeds) in Upper Cretaceous. *Meddelelser fra Dansk Geologisk Forening, 15*, 556–558.

Margara, J. (1946). Existence de zoothylacies chez des clypeastres (echinodermes) de l'helvetien du Proche-Orient. *Bulletin du Muséum National d'Histoire Naturelle, Paris, 18*, 423–427.

Marshall, B., & Bouchet, P. (2015). Eulimidae Philippi, 1853. *MolluscaBase (2015). World Register of Marine Species.* www.marinespecies.org/aphia .php.

Martinelli Filho, J. E., dos Santos, R. B., & Ribeiro, C. C. (2014). Host selection, host-use pattern and competition in *Dissodactylus crinitichelis* and *Clypeasterophilus stebbingi* (Brachyura: Pinnotheridae). *Symbiosis, 63* (3), 99–110.

Matsuda, H., Hamano, T., & Nagasawa, K. (2013). Growth and reproductive cycle of *Hypermastus tokunagai* (Caenogastropoda: Eulimidae), an ectoparasite of the sand dollar *Scaphechinus mirabilis* (Clypeasteroida: Scutellidae) in the Seto Inland Sea, Japan. *Journal of the Marine Biological Association of the United Kingdom, 93*(4), 1041–1051.

Matsuda, H., Hamano, T., Yamamoto, K.-i., & Hori, S. (2008). Ecological study of *Hypermastus tokunagai* (Gastropoda: Eulimidae), parasitic on the sand dollar *Scaphechinus mirabilis* (Echinoidea: Irregularia). *Venus*, *66*(3–4), 205–216.

Matsuda, H., Uyeno, D., & Nagasawa, K. (2010). A new species of *Hypermastus* (Prosobranchia: Eulimidae) associated with *Echinodiscus tenuissimus* (Echinoidea: Astriclypeidae) from off Okinawa, Japan. *Venus*, *69*(1), 17.

McClanahan, T. (1999). Predation and the control of the sea urchin *Echinometra viridis* and fleshy algae in the patch reefs of Glovers Reef, Belize. *Ecosystems*, *2*(6), 511–523.

McClintock, J. B., & Marion, K. R. (1993). Predation by the king helmet (*Cassis tuberosa*) on six-holed sand dollars (*Leodia sexiesperforata*) at San Salvador, Bahamas. *Bulletin of Marine Science*, *52*(3), 1013–1017.

McNamara, K. J. (1994). The significance of gastropod predation to patterns of evolution and extinction in Australian Tertiary echinoids. In Guille, D., Féral, J.-P., & Roux, M., eds., *Echinoderms through Time*. Rotterdam: CRC Press, pp. 785–793.

McPherson, B. (1968). Contributions to the biology of the sea urchin *Eucidaris tribuloides* (Lamarck). *Bulletin of Marine Science*, *18*(2), 400–443.

McRoberts, C. A. (2001). Triassic bivalves and the initial Marine Mesozoic Revolution: A role for predators? *Geology*, *29*(4), 359–362.

Meadows, C. A., Fordyce, R. E., & Baumiller, T. K. (2015). Drill holes in the irregular echinoid, *Fibularia*, from the Oligocene of New Zealand. *Palaios*, *30*(12), 810–817.

Mehl, J., Mehl, D., & Häckel, W. (1991). Parasitäre Zystenbildungen an Jurassischen Cidariden und das Porospongia-Problem. *Berliner Geowissenschaftliche Abhandlungen A*, *134*, 227–261.

Merrill, R. J., & Hobson, E. S. (1970). Field observations of *Dendraster excentricus*, a sand dollar of western North America. *American Midland Naturalist*, *83*(2), 595–624.

Mifsud, C. (1990). Two eulimid species parasitizing the echinoid sea urchin *Cidaris cidaris* (L., 1758). *La Conchiglia Roma*, *22*(258), 30.

Moore, D. R. (1956). Observation on predation of echinoderms by three species of Cassidae. *The Nautilus*, *69*, 73–76.

Nebelsick, J. H. (2020). Ecology of clypeasteroids. In *Developments in Aquaculture and Fisheries Science*. Elsevier, Vol. 43, pp. 315–331.

Nebelsick, J., & Kampfer, S. (1994). Taphonomy of *Clypeaster humilis* and *Echinodiscus auritus* from the Red Sea. In Guille, D., Féral, J.-P., & Roux, M., eds., *Echinoderms through Time*. Rotterdam: Balkema, pp. 803–808.

Nebelsick, J. H., & Kowalewski, M. (1999). Drilling predation on recent clypeasteroid echinoids from the Red Sea. *Palaios*, *14*(2), 127–144.

Nebelsick, J. H., & Mancosu, A. (2022). Fish predation on *Clypeaster humilis* from the Red Sea: Potential for recognition in the fossil record. *Contributions from the Museum of Paleontology, University of Michigan*, *34*(11), 148–157.

Nebelsick, J. H., Carnevali, C., & Bonasoro, F. (1998). Taphonomic legacy of predation on echinoids. In Carnevali, M. D. C., & Francesco, B., eds., *Echinoderm Research 1998: Proceedings of the Fifth European Conference on Echinoderms*. Milan, pp. 347–352.

Nebelsick, J. (1999). Taphonomic comparison between Recent and fossil sand dollars. *Palaeogeography, Palaeoclimatology, Palaeoecology*, *149*(1–4), 349–358.

Neumann, C., & Hampe, O. (2018). Eggs for breakfast? Analysis of a probable mosasaur biting trace on the Cretaceous echinoid *Echinocorys ovata* Leske, 1778. *Fossil Record*, *21*(1), 55–66.

Neumann, C., & Wisshak, M. (2006). A foraminiferal parasite on the sea urchin *Echinocorys*: Ichnological evidence from the Late Cretaceous (Lower Maastrichtian, Northern Germany). *Ichnos*, *13*(3), 185–190.

Neumann, C., & Wisshak, M. (2009). Gastropod parasitism on Late Cretaceous to early Paleocene holasteroid echinoids – Evidence from *Oichnus halo* isp. n. *Palaeogeography, Palaeoclimatology, Palaeoecology*, *284*(3–4), 115–119.

Oliverio, M., Buzzurro, G., & Villa, R. (1994). A new eulimid gastropod from the eastern Mediterranean Sea (Caenogastropoda, Ptenoglossa). *Bollettino Malacologico*, *30*(5–9), 211–215.

Pastorino, R. S. G., & Zelaya, D. G. (2001). A new species of the eulimid genus *Pelseneeria* Koehler & Vaney, 1908 (Mollusca: Gastropoda) from Staten Island, Argentina. *The Veliger*, *44*(3), 310–314.

Pearse, J. S., & Cameron, R. A. (1991). Echinodermata: Echinoidea. In Giese, A. C., Pearse, J. S., & Pearse, V. B., eds., *Reproduction of Marine Invertebrates. Vol. 6: Echinoderms and Lophophorates*. Pacific Grove: Boxwood Press, pp. 513–662.

Petsios, E., Portell, R. W., Farrar, L. et al. (2021). An asynchronous Mesozoic Marine Revolution: The Cenozoic intensification of predation on echinoids. *Proceedings of the Royal Society B*, *288*(1947), 20210400.

Philippi, (1845). *Arch. Naturg. Jhg. 11*(1), 355.

Pilsbry, H. (1956). A gastropod domiciliary in sea urchin spines. *The Nautilus*, *69*(4), 109–110.

Poulin, R. (2011). Evolutionary ecology of parasites. In Poulin, R., ed., *Evolutionary Ecology of Parasites*. Princeton: Princeton University Press.

Powers, L. W. (1977). A catalogue and bibliography to the crabs (Brachyura) of the Gulf of Mexico. *Contributions to Marine Science, 20*(supplement), 1–190.

Prouho, H. (1887). *Reserches sur le Dorocidaris papillata et quelques autres &chinides de la MediterranCe. Archs Zool, 15,* 213–380.

Prouho, H. (1888). *Recherches sur le Dorocidaris papillata et quelques autres échinides de la Méditerranée; Propositions données par la faculté (No. 103).* Paris: Typographie A. Hennuyer.

Queiroz, V. (2020). An unprecedented association of an encrusting bryozoan on the test of a live sea urchin: Epibiotic relationship and physiological responses. *Marine Biodiversity, 50*(5), 1–7.

Queiroz, V., Neves, E., Sales, L., & Johnsson, R. (2017). The gall-former *Sabinella troglodytes* (Caenogastropoda: Eulimidae) and its association with *Eucidaris tribuloides* (Echinodermata: Echinoidea). *Journal of Conchology, 42*(5), 371–377.

Quinn, B. G. (1965). Predation in sea urchins. *Bulletin of Marine Science, 15*(1), 259–264.

Radwanska, U., & Poirot, E. (2010). Copepod-infested Bathonian (Middle Jurassic) echinoids from northern France. *Acta Geologica Polonica, 60*(4), 549–555.

Radwańska, U., & Radwański, A. (2005). Myzostomid and copepod infestation of Jurassic echinoderms: A general approach, some new occurrences, and/or re-interpretation of previous reports. *Acta Geologica Polonica, 55*(2), 109–130.

Rinaldi, A. C., & Malacologico, B. (1994). Frequency and distribution of *Vitreolina philippi* (De Rayneval and Ponzi, 1854) (Prosobranchia, Eulimidae) on two regular echinoid species found along the southern coast of Sardinia. *Bollettino Malacologico, 30,* 29–32.

Rodríguez, M., Pérez-Dionis, G., & Barquin, J. (2001). Eulimid gastropods (Caenogastropoda: Eulimidae) of the Canary Islands. *Part II. Species parasiting the crinoid Antedon bifida. Iberus, 19*(1), 25–35.

Roman, J. (1954). Sur le genre Echinolampas. *Bulletin de la Société Géologique de France, 6*(7–9), 689–699.

Salazar, A., & Reyes Bonilla, H. (1998). Parasitismo de *Thyca callista* (Gastropoda: Capulidae) sobre *Phataria unifascialis* (Asteroidea: Ophidiasteridae) en el Golfo de California, México. *Revista de Biología Tropical, 46*(3), 833–836.

Sales, L., & Queiroz, V. (2021). Sexual dimorphism in the parasitic snail *Nanobalcis worsfoldi*: A histological and morphometric approach with insights for the family Eulimidae. *Canadian Journal of Zoology, 99*(11), 995–1001.

Sarasúa, H., & Espinosa, J. (1977). Dos especies nuevas del género *Prunum* (Mollusca: Marginellidae). Instituto de Zoologia, Academia de Ciencias de Cuba. *Poeyana, 173*, 1–5.

Schiaparelli, S., Ghirardo, C., Bohn, J. et al. (2007). Antarctic associations: The parasitic relationship between the gastropod *Bathycrinicola tumidula* (Thiele, 1912) (Ptenoglossa: Eulimidae) and the comatulid *Notocrinus virilis* Mortensen, 1917 (Crinoidea: Notocrinidae) in the Ross Sea. *Polar Biology, 30*(12), 1545–1555.

Schmitt, W. L. (1973). Decapoda I, Brachyura I, family Pinnotheridae. *Crustaceorum Catalogus, 3*, 1–160.

Schneider, C. L. (2003). Hitchhiking on Pennsylvanian echinoids: Epibionts on *Archaeocidaris*. *Palaios, 18*(4–5), 435–444.

Schneider, C. L., Sprinkle, J., & Ryder, D. (2005). Pennsylvanian (Late Carboniferous) echinoids from the Winchell Formation, north-central Texas, USA. *Journal of Paleontology, 79*(4), 745–762.

Serafy, K. D. (1979). Echinoids (Echinodermata: Echinoidea). *Memoirs of the Hourglass Cruises, 5*(3), 1–120. Florida Department of Natural Resources.

Sievers, D., Friedrich, J. P., & Nebelsick, J. H. (2014). A feast for crows: Bird predation on irregular echinoids from Brittany, France. *Palaios, 29*(3), 87–94.

Sievers, D., & Nebelsick, J. H. (2018). Fish predation on a Mediterranean echinoid: Identification and preservation potential. *Palaios, 33*(2), 47–54.

Signor, P. W., & Brett, C. E. (1984). The mid-Paleozoic precursor to the Mesozoic Marine Revolution. *Paleobiology, 10*(2), 229–245.

Simonelli, V. (1889). *Terreni e fossili dell'Isola di Pianosa nel Mar Tirreno*. London: Tipografia nazionale.

Smith, A. (1984). *Echinoid Palaeobiology: Special Topics in Palaeontology*. Londres, Inglaterra: George Allen & Unwin, pp. 170–173.

Smith, B. J. (1990). Superfamily Eulimoidea. In Beesley, P. L., Ross, G. J. B., & Wells, A., eds., *Mollusca the Southern Synthesis.Fauna of Australia*. Vol. 5. Melbourne: CSIRO Publishing, pp. 817–818.

Sohl, N. F. (1964). Neogastropoda, Opisthobranchia and Basommatophora from the Ripley, Owl Creek, and Prairie Bluff formations. *Geological Survey Professional Paper 331B*, 153–344.

Solovyev, A. (1961). The parasite *Canceripustula nocens* in a Late Jurassic echinoid. *Paleontologitchesky Zhurnal, 4*, 115–119.

Sonnenholzner, J., & Lawrence, J. (1998). Disease and predation in *Encope micropora* (Echinoidea: Clypeasteroida) at Playas, Ecuador. In Mooi, R., & Telford, M., eds., *Echinoderms: San Francisco. Proceedings of 9th*

International Echinoderm Conference, San Francisco. Rotterdam : A. A. Balkema, 829–883.

Sonnenholzner, J., & Molina, L. (2005). Parasitic eulimids gastropods in echinoderms of the Islas Galápagos, Ecuador. *Festivus, 37*, 85–88.

Sonnenholzner, J. I., Lafferty, K. D., & Ladah, L. B. (2011). Food webs and fishing affect parasitism of the sea urchin *Eucidaris galapagensis* in the Galápagos. *Ecology, 92*(12), 2276–2284.

Stock, J. H. (1968). The Calvocheridae, a family of copepods inducing galls in sea-urchin spines. *Bijdragen tot de Dierkunde, 38*(1), 85–90.

Stock, J. H., & Gooding, R. U. (1986). A new siphonostomatoid copepod associated with the West Indian sea urchin, *Diadema antillarum*. *Bulletin of Marine Science, 39*(1), 102–109.

Tackett, L. S. (2016). Late Triassic durophagy and the origin of the Mesozoic marine revolution. *Palaios, 31*(4), 122–124.

Takano, T., & Kano, Y. (2014). Molecular phylogenetic investigations of the relationships of the echinoderm-parasite family Eulimidae within Hypsogastropoda (Mollusca). *Molecular Phylogenetics and Evolution, 79*, 258–269.

Takano, T., Kimura, S., & Kano, Y. (2020). Host identification for the deep-sea snail genus *Haliella* with description of a new species (Caenogastropoda, Eulimidae). *ZooKeys, 908*, 19–30.

Takeda, S., Tamura, S., & Washio, M. (1997). Relationship between the pea crab *Pinnixa tumida* and its endobenthic holothurian host *Paracaudina chilensis*. *Marine Ecology Progress Series, 149*, 143–154.

Tegner, M., & Levin, L. (1983). Spiny lobsters and sea urchins: Analysis of a predator-prey interaction. *Journal of Experimental Marine Biology and Ecology, 73*(2), 125–150.

Telford, M. (1982). Echinoderm spine structure, feeding and host relationships of four species of *Dissodactylus* (Brachyura: Pinnotheridae). *Bulletin of Marine Science, 32*(2), 584–594.

Thiele, J. (1925). Gastropoda der Deutschen Tiefsee-Expedition. II Teil. *Wissenschaftliche Ergebnisse der Deutschen Tiefsee-Expedition auf dem Dampher "Valdivia" 1898–1899, 17*(2), 35–382, pls. 313–346.

Thoma, B. P., Heard, R. W., & Felder, D. L. (2009). Redescription of *Pinnixa arenicola* Rathbun, 1922 (Decapoda: Brachyura: Pinnotheridae), with new observations on its range and host. *Proceedings of the Biological Society of Washington, 122*(1), 72–80.

Thoma, B. P., Heard, R. W., & Vargas, R. (2005). A new species of *Parapinnixa* (Decapoda: Brachyura: Pinnotheridae) from Isla del Coco, Costa Rica. *Proceedings of the Biological Society of Washington, 118*(3), 543–550.

Tyler, C. L., Dexter, T. A., Portell, R. W., & Kowalewski, M. (2018). Predation-facilitated preservation of echinoids in a tropical marine environment. *Palaios*, *33*(10), 478–486.

Vaïtilingon, D., Eeckhaut, I., Fourgon, D., & Jangoux, M. (2004). Population dynamics, infestation and host selection of *Vexilla vexillum*, an ectoparasitic muricid of echinoids, in Madagascar. *Diseases of Aquatic Organisms*, *61*(3), 241–255.

Van Valen, L. (1973). A new evolutionary law. *Evolutionary Theory*, *1*, 1–30.

Venmathi Maran, B. A., Kim, I.-H., Bratova, O. A., & Ivanenko, V. N. (2017). Two new species of poecilostomatoid copepods symbiotic on the venomous echinoid *Toxopneustes pileolus* (Lamarck) (Echinodermata) from Vietnam. *Systematic Parasitology*, *94*(2), 227–241.

Vermeij, G. J. (1977). The Mesozoic marine revolution: Evidence from snails, predators and grazers. *Paleobiology*, *3*, 245–258.

Vermeij, G. J. (1983). Shell-breaking predation through time. In Tevesz, M. J. S., & McCall, P. L., eds., *Biotic Interactions in Recent and Fossil Benthic Communities*. New York: Plenum, pp. 649–669.

Vermeij, G. J. (1987). *Evolution and Escalation: An Ecological History of Life*. Princeton: Princeton University Press, p. 527.

Vidal-Martinez, V. M., Pech, D., Sures, B., Purucker, S. T., & Poulin, R. (2010). Can parasites really reveal environmental impact? *Trends in Parasitology*, *26*(1), 44–51.

Warén, A. (1980a). Revision of the genera *Thyca*, *Stilifer*, *Scalenostoma*, *Mucronalia* and *Echineulima* (Mollusca, Prosobranchia, Eulimidae). *Zoologica Scripta*, *9*(1–4), 187–210.

Warén, A. (1980b). Descriptions of new taxa of Eulimidae (Mollusca, Prosobranchia), with notes on some previously described genera. *Zoologica Scripta*, *9*(1–4), 283–306.

Warén, A. (1981a). Eulimid gastropods parasitic on echinoderms in the New Zealand region. *New Zealand Journal of Zoology*, *8*(3), 313–324.

Warén, A. (1981b). Revision of the genera *Apicalia* A. Adams and *Stilapex* Iredale and description of two new genera (Mollusca, Prosobranchia, Eulimidae). *Zoologica Scripta*, *10*(2), 133–154.

Warén, A. (1983). A generic revision of the family Eulimidae (Gastropoda, Prosobranchia). *Journal of Molluscan Studies*, *49*(Supplement 13), 1–96.

Warén, A. (1992). Comments on and descriptions of eulimid gastropods from tropical West America. *The Veliger*, *35*(3), 177–194.

Warén, A., & Crossland, M. (1991). Revision of *Hypermastus* Pilsbry, 1899 and Turveria Berry, 1956 (Gastropoda: Prosobranchia: Eulimidae), two genera parasitic on sand dollars. *Records of the Australian Museum*, *43*(1), 85–112.

Warén, A., & Mifsud, C. (1990). *Nanobalcis*, a new eulimid genus (Prosobranchia) parasitic on cidaroid sea urchins, with two new species, and comments on *Sabinella bonifaciae* (Nordsieck). *Bolletino Malacologico, 26*(1–4), 37–46.

Warén, A., & Moolenbeek, R. (1989). A new eulimid gastropod, *Trochostilifer eucidaricola*, parasitic on the pencil urchin *Eucidaris tribuloides* from the southern Caribbean. *Proceedings of the Biological Society of Washington, 102*(1), 169–175.

Warén, A., Norris, D., & Templado, J. (1994). Descriptions of four new eulimid gastropods parasitic on irregular sea urchins. *The Veliger, 37*(2), 141–154.

Weihe, S. C., & Gray, I. (1968). Observations on the biology of the sand dollar *Mellita quinquiesperforata* (Leske). *Journal of the Elisha Mitchell Scientific Society, 84*(2), 315–327.

Will, I. (2009). Host preference, detection, and dependence: The ectoparasitic gastropods *Melanella acicula* and *Peasistilifer nitidula* (Eulimidae) on holothurian hosts. *UCB Moorea Class: Biology and Geomorphology of Tropical Islands – Student Research Papers, Fall 2009.* Berkeley: University of California.

Williams, A. B. (1984). *Shrimps, Lobsters, and Crabs of the Atlantic Coast of the Eastern United States, Maine to Florida.* Washington, DC: Smithsonian Institution Press, p. 550.

Wilson, M. A., Borszcz, T., & Zatoń, M. (2014). Bitten spines reveal unique evidence for fish predation on Middle Jurassic echinoids. *Lethaia, 48*(1), 4–9.

Wirtz, P., de Melo, G., & de Grave, S. (2009). Symbioses of decapod crustaceans along the coast of Espírito Santo, Brazil. *Marine Biodiversity Records, 2*, 1–9.

Wisshak, M., & Neumann, C. (2006). A symbiotic association of a boring polychaete and an echinoid from the Late Cretaceous of Germany. *Acta Palaeontologica Polonica, 51*(3), 589–597.

Wisshak, M., & Neumann, C. (2020). Dead urchin walking: Resilience of an arctic *Strongylocentrotus* to severe skeletal damage. *Polar Biology, 43*(4), 391–396.

Wisshak, M., Neumann, C., Sanna, G., Nielsen, K. S., & Milàn, J. (2023). Suspected foraminiferan parasitism on a Late Cretaceous echinoid host recorded by the new attachment trace fossil *Solichnus aestheticus. Acta Palaeontologica Polonica, 68* (*in press*), 13–22.

Yamamori, L., & Kato, M. (2020). Shift of feeding mode in an epizoic stalked barnacle inducing gall formation of host sea urchin. *Iscience, 23*(3), 100885.

Ying, M. L. S. (2017). Parasitic snails, *Vitreobalcis* sp., on white sea urchins at Cyrene Reef. *Singapore Biodiversity Records, 2017*, 123–124.

Zamora, S., Mayoral, E., Vintaned, J. A. G., Bajo, S., & Espílez, E. (2008). The infaunal echinoid *Micraster*: Taphonomic pathways indicated by sclerozoan trace and body fossils from the Upper Cretaceous of northern Spain. *Geobios*, *41*(1), 15–29.

Zinsmeister, W. J. (1980). Observations on the predation of the clypeasteroid echinoid, *Monophoraster darwini*, from the upper Miocene Entrerrios Formation, Patagonia, Argentina. *Journal of Paleontology*, *54*(5), 910–912.

Złotnik, M., & Ceranka, T. (2005a). Patterns of drilling predation of cassid gastropods preying on echinoids from the middle Miocene of Poland. *Acta Palaeontologica Polonica*, *50*(3), 409–428.

Złotnik, M., & Ceranka, T. (2005b). Traces of cassid snails predation upon the echinoids from the middle Miocene of Poland. *Acta Palaeontologica Polonica*, *50*, 633–634.

Acknowledgments

We thank Troy Dexter (Gerace Research Centre), Edward Stanley (FLMNH Digital Imaging Division), Gordon Hendler and Austin Hendy (both LANHM), John Slapcinsky, Sean Roberts (both FLMNH), Paul Larson and Corinne Fuchs (both FFWCC), and Nathan Wright (Baylor University) for either assistance in the field, collections, or specimen imaging. We also thank the numerous contributors and editors of the Paleobiology Database (paleobiodb.org) and the Global Biodiversity Information Facility (gbif.org). This work was supported by a National Science Foundation grant to Tyler and Kowalewski (EAR SGP-1630475 and EAR SGP-1630276).

Cambridge Elements ☰

Elements of Paleontology

Editor-in-Chief

Colin D. Sumrall
University of Tennessee

About the Series

The Elements of Paleontology series is a publishing collaboration between the Paleontological Society and Cambridge University Press. The series covers the full spectrum of topics in paleontology and paleobiology, and related topics in the Earth and life sciences of interest to students and researchers of paleontology.

The Paleontological Society is an international nonprofit organization devoted exclusively to the science of paleontology: invertebrate and vertebrate paleontology, micropaleontology, and paleobotany. The Society's mission is to advance the study of the fossil record through scientific research, education, and advocacy. Its vision is to be a leading global advocate for understanding life's history and evolution. The Society has several membership categories, including regular, amateur/avocational, student, and retired. Members, representing some 40 countries, include professional paleontologists, academicians, science editors, Earth science teachers, museum specialists, undergraduate and graduate students, postdoctoral scholars, and amateur/avocational paleontologists.

Paleontological
S O C I E T Y

Cambridge Elements $\equiv$

Elements of Paleontology

Printed in the United States
by Baker & Taylor Publisher Services